Prayer

Prayer the Churches banquet, Angels age,
   Gods breath in man returning to his birth,
   The soul in paraphrase, heart in pilgrimage,
The Christian plummet sounding heav'n and earth;

Engine against th' Almightie, sinners towre,
   Reversed thunder, Christ-side-piercing spear,
   The six-daies world-transposing in an houre,
A kinde of tune, which all things heare and fear;

Softnesse, and peace, and joy, and love, and blisse,
   Exalted Manna, gladnesse of the best,
   Heaven in ordinarie, man well drest,
The milkie way, the bird of Paradise,

   Church-bels beyond the starres heard, the souls blood,
   The land of spices; something understood.

GEORGE HERBERT

D1422079

Something Understood

A companion to
Celebrating Common Prayer

Something Understood

A companion to
Celebrating Common Prayer

Edited by Paul Roberts,
David Stancliffe
and Kenneth Stevenson

Hodder & Stoughton
LONDON SYDNEY AUCKLAND

British Library Cataloguing in Publication Data

A catalogue record for this book is available from the British Library

ISBN 0-340-58915-9

Published by Hodder and Stoughton, a division of Hodder and Stoughton Ltd, Mill Road, Dunton Green, Sevenoaks, Kent TN13 2YA.
Editorial Office: 47 Bedford Square, London WC1B 3DP.

Photoset by Rowland Phototypesetting Ltd, Bury St Edmunds, Suffolk

Printed in Great Britain by Cox and Wyman Ltd, Reading, Berks

Contents

Something Understood

The fundamental purpose of *Celebrating Common Prayer – The Daily Office SSF* is this: to help the Church as a whole to pray together daily in a reflective and structured way.

This was always Cranmer's intention in the Book of Common Prayer. Although his version of Morning and Evening Prayer has long provided a non-eucharistic form of worship on Sundays and has done much thereby to characterise Anglican public worship, it has only rather patchily achieved his other purpose of being the regular worship attended by the whole congregation and offered day by day in parish churches throughout the land.

For many regular Sunday churchgoers, personal prayer during the week is unstructured and haphazard. This places even more burdens on the Sunday act of worship, which has to perform the task of nourishing and sustaining reflective prayer during the week, as well as celebrating and proclaiming the risen life of Christ in word and sacrament. A pattern of daily prayer which complements eucharistic worship, such as *Celebrating Common Prayer*, offers a major resource to the Church. I hope that many Christians will use it to engage in a pattern of daily common prayer which will unite us all in prayer and praise, and allow us to feed on a common diet of psalmody and canticle.

Since the publication of *The Alternative Service Book 1980*, our knowledge of the origin and purpose of daily common prayer in the early Church has grown enormously. As a result, many people long for a return to a simpler and more celebratory form of common prayer for our time.

In *Celebrating Common Prayer*, a large number of contributors have helped the Society of Saint Francis to respond to this longing, and to offer to the Church a pattern of daily prayer which meets needs expressed by Christians from a wide variety of traditions. This book tells the story of the enterprise, and allows a number of the contributors to reflect on the way in which a common concern to re-establish such a pattern led to their co-operation in the publication of *Celebrating Common Prayer*.

CCP contains a simple structure for Morning and Evening Prayer, when desired. The services can be led as effectively by lay people as the clergy. There is an emphasis on celebrating together rather than "saying the Office" as a private and exclusively clerical obligation. It also makes suggestions as to how the services might be celebrated in a wide range of circumstances. The use of music of different styles, and of a visual focus – the Bible, a lighted candle, a large cross, for example – will enrich the worship for many.

Although the services are conceived for corporate use, they can of course be adapted easily so that people may use them when alone. We need to recognise too that there are many occasions when people may have need of a structured form of prayer when they are on their own, whether it is in hospital or on a commuter train, those peculiar forms of isolation when there are many other people around. It is in these situations as well as in other more corporate gatherings that *Celebrating Common Prayer* will help us to know that we are sharing fully in the Church's prayer.

It is this – the recovery of a joyful partnership in common prayer – which is at the heart of the welcome proposal which this book introduces and describes.

✠ GEORGE CANTUAR
Lambeth Palace,
London

Celebrating Common Prayer – A New Point of Departure

The end of the 1970s marked a watershed for the history of liturgical renewal. Most churches had produced modern language services which incorporated the insights gained over at least half a century of liturgical research and experimentation. In many places today, this generation of service books is being re-revised, but today's revisers need to be more precise in their justification for proposing any radical changes, lest they fall foul of the charge of "tampering with the liturgy again". It is therefore important that a new piece of liturgy on the scale of *Celebrating Common Prayer* should be accompanied by some explanation of the principles underlying its composition, and why it was deemed necessary to produce a new Daily Office when relatively modern texts are already available.

Of all the services of *The Alternative Service Book 1980*, those of the Daily Office had altered least from the Book of Common Prayer. This was, in part, deliberate: the Anglican Church has a unique relationship with the Daily Office, brought about by the failure of Cranmer and other reformers to reinstate a weekly communicating Eucharist as the central act of Sunday worship. Instead, the Morning and Evening Prayer offices became the staple Sunday diet of most Anglican worshippers until the present century. For the creators of the ASB, alteration of the Morning and Evening Prayer provision would have had a major impact upon a central element in the tradition of Sunday worship in Anglican churches, even as late as 1980.

Yet when Thomas Cranmer was drafting the services of Morning and Evening Prayer, he was preparing a *Daily* Office, not a central provision for Sunday non-sacramental worship. There are many ways in which services of a Daily Office do not fit a weekly context; for example, in the difficulties weekly congregations have in singing non-metrical psalmody. This has never been more apparent than in the present day, when many churches have abandoned the provisions of the ASB, or drastically modified them into Family Services or other flexible formats. In the current round of liturgical revision, the Liturgical Commission of the Church of England has sought to address this by devising a distinct route for non-sacramental Sunday worship called the "Service of the Word". Proposals for this were set out in *Patterns for Worship* (1989). Such changes free the Daily Office in the Church of England to address the specific issues of daily prayer, without needing to have one eye on the requirements of Sunday non-sacramental services.

What, then, are the issues facing Daily Office provision today? The first has been with us for a long time: most people (clergy, usually, excepted) do not use it at all. Indeed, the "once a week" Sunday pattern of Morning and Evening Prayer marked a falling short of Cranmer's initial intentions, as he clearly hoped that most people (clergy and laity) would participate in the Morning and Evening Prayer on a daily, rather than a weekly basis. The ASB provision attempted to address a number of problems which stood in the way of wider use. The "Shorter Forms" of Morning and Evening Prayer marked a step forward, and the Psalter was arranged to reduce the number of psalm verses said. Yet these services, reflecting the conservatism of the revision, succeed more in trimming back than in providing genuine flexibility, while they offer very little variety. For the person or group considering using the Daily Office, the ASB provision looks an unpromising diet to follow, day in, day out.

Secondly, most Christians do not consider the Daily Office as central to the life of Christian prayer. Indeed, it would be wrong to assume that people are convinced of the need for a Daily Office at all. Underlying the production of *Celebrating Common Prayer* is a shared conviction that the Daily Office is a vital ingredient in revitalising the prayer of the whole Church today. In considering the prayer of people in recent years, it is apparent that most Christians find prayer difficult in modern life, partly due to the pressure of time and distractions, but also because prayer is an almost forgotten skill which is seldom taught – taught simply – even to people new to the faith. Most are simply left to "get on with it" outside the boundaries of Sunday worship. A suitably flexible provision of Daily Office has the double benefit of giving people words to frame their prayer, and encouragement to pray together (or alone) regularly in ways which are compatible with modern lifestyles.

Thirdly, although many experience difficulties in praying, there is an explosion of interest in Christian spirituality and contemplative prayer. This is a welcome response from Christians living in an increasingly materialistic culture. Yet the life of contemplation needs a grounding in the Daily Office to achieve balance and fruitfulness, as we see in the lives of all the great teachers on prayer. Without such grounding, a person's developing prayer life is in danger of becoming too individualistic and subjective. As Kenneth Leech says,

> The value of an Office is its objectivity. It is a means by which we pray with the whole Church, uniting our prayer with that of millions of other Christians living and dead. This is true whether one is alone or with a group, for the Office is essentially a corporate act. (*True Prayer*, London: Sheldon Press, 1980. p190)

Celebrating Common Prayer seeks to meet the need for an Office which unites the many varied situations of the members of the whole Christian community. Its basic structure is simple and adaptable, and can be expanded from an outline used in a basic rule of prayer, to the more complex requirements of religious communities. It is thus a uniting rite which illustrates and serves the spiritual unity of the Daily Office.

The principal features of flexibility and variety reflected in the book arise from new insights in liturgical scholarship over recent decades. Today it is possible to see something of the Daily Office in its earliest formative historical period. The impression given is that the main roots of the Office lie in a discipline of corporate praise and intercessory prayer offered by the whole people of God, and centred on two major gatherings in the morning and the evening. Later developments, often arising from monastic practice (but not exclusively so), can be judged against this basic norm, and an assessment of where initially peripheral elements came to over-dominate in the course of time. From such study, some interesting and useful features emerge. For example, the Office in recent years may be judged to be excessively clericalised (almost to the point of being bizarre). In the Anglican Office especially, scripture reading has predominated to a degree which swamps the simpler task of praising God and praying for those in need. Moreover, recent study has also shown the wide diversity of forms which the Daily Office has taken across time, many of which were very flexible and centred on the prayers of lay Christians, rather than the more structured forms used in religious communities and by clergy.

The assessments of historical scholarship, and the emergence of new patterns of Sunday worship mentioned above together indicate that the Daily Office in the Anglican tradition is set for a new point of departure. *Celebrating Common Prayer* draws these insights together into a Daily Office book for everyone. The two major foci of Morning and Evening Prayer are presented first in their fully developed forms, and then in their essential structure which is illustrated by the presentation of a form of the "Simple Celebration". Adaptation and creative experiment is actively encouraged once an essential grasp of the structures has been achieved. In addition, a wealth of canticles from Scripture and beyond is compiled for varying use. The unfolding pattern of the week gives a sense of rotation and repetition without unholy drudgery. This enlivens the use of the Psalter where canticles and psalms are loosely linked to give each Office cohesion with variety. The Office of Compline contains much that will be familiar, but links in with the structures of the other hours to form part of the whole.

The Midday Office has its own unique flavour, and may prove one of the most creative innovations of the book. Its particular focus on the secular arena provides a welcome antidote to much churchiness and isolationism in modern popular spiritualities. The apparent paradox of this idea arising from a religious community will not be so great to those who know the Franciscan spirituality which inspires it. Users of the Office now have an opportunity to share in a prayer model which has its heart with God and two feet on the ground.

The best way to understand a Daily Office is to use it. We hope that in the course of their praying, people will find their own way of using *Celebrating Common Prayer* which is realistic to their needs. Nevertheless, some understanding of the inner reasoning of the various sections of the book will be helpful, especially to leaders who wish to adapt it for use by groups and communities. It is to this task of further explanation that the present book is dedicated, in the knowledge that our own efforts in writing prayer for the people of God only come to fruition through the empowering, creative Spirit at work in his praying Church. For that we pray.

PAUL ROBERTS

1 ◆ Daily prayer: a brief history

George Guiver

Most Christians pray regularly, many will read or write books on the subject of prayer and some offer teaching and guidance on it. Prayer, people believe, is an immediate thing, an act of conversing with God as an individual. But historically prayer has been very different, and it is time for a rediscovery of its true nature. A brief journey through the Church's history is illuminating.

This history begins with Jesus. There can be little doubt that Jesus and his followers prayed every day. The Jews had a very rich religious culture and it would not have been possible for a Jew in the first century to pass a day without praying to God. Jesus would have been taught by his parents to pray at three set times in the day as well as at other times of day, at meals for example. The prayers would have been familiar ones, ingrained in the memory through repetition. When Jesus' disciples asked him how they should pray, he gave various answers. He said that prayer should be persistent and repeated (Lk 18.1–8); not using vain repetitions, but sincere ones (Mt 6.7); he gave his followers at least one set form, the Lord's Prayer (Mt 6.9–15), and he set an example by making time to pray (Lk 5.16). People in ancient times had very little experience of privacy, and most "private" prayer would have been in the family. When Jesus talked to people who lived in small, one-roomed houses about going into a private room to pray (Mt 6.6), he was being sarcastic about those who made a show of praying. Jesus' point has often been misunderstood to mean that prayer should be an utterly personal, private thing: such an understanding would have been alien to him and to his contemporaries. We need to forget the modern idea of a "private" life and individuality, if we are to understand that the whole of life in New Testament times, including prayer, was soaked in a sense of community.

The early Christians were able to build on this rich

spiritual heritage and the book of Acts tells us that they too observed set hours of prayer each day at the third, sixth and ninth hours (Ac 2.15; 10.9; 3.1; 10.30), and generally the picture is one of Christians praying together rather than alone. Unlike today, the apostles were blessed in that they did not pray out of a vacuum. They were not empty but full, entranced by the bright light of the resurrection. Every waking hour was filled with this radiance, every Sunday was for them an Easter. In baptism and in the Eucharist, the Lord's cross and resurrection were truly present (Ro 6.4; 1 Co 11.26), and believers knew themselves to be so enveloped and united in this mystery that they were one Body, the mystical Body of the Church.

As a result, they also knew that prayer was not simply a product of their own efforts, it was the Spirit of Christ praying in them, moving in their hearts, so that they could cry "Abba" to the Father (Ro 8.15; Gal 4.6). Prayer was so rich with the presence of Christ in the heart of the believer, and within the company of the believers, that Paul could say: "I no longer live, but Christ lives in me" (Gal 2.20).

This sense of being part of a rich religious culture shared by the whole Church, and alive with the presence of Christ, is largely lost today. Praying now seems to be a personal and not always successful struggle to get through to God who is very distant. Such an evaluation of prayer and praying cannot be reconciled with the history of prayer and should not be read back into New Testament experience.

In the centuries immediately following New Testament times, this rich religious culture remained. People continued to pray at set times so that even if they prayed alone or in their own houses, they were still praying with the Church. An example of this can be found in the household practice of evening prayer, the lighting of the lamps ("Lucernarium"). This was a daily ritual of hymns and prayers, which took place at the day's turning-point when people celebrated the light of Christ in their lives.

By the time of the fourth century and the new freedom of the Church under Constantine, a further development had taken place: so strong was the Christian sense of the Body of Christ that people naturally began to celebrate these daily times of prayer in the church in preference to their own homes. All over the Christian world the practice grew of going to church every day before work for a short service, and again in the evening when work was done. These services, the ancestors of our Matins and Evensong, were very different from many people's perceptions of Morning and Evening Prayer. They were performed with an appealing degree of razzmatazz and imaginative flair, something more like "Songs of Praise" than a said service. The clergy processed in, there were candles and incense, the choir sang with gusto and the music was rousing. The content was very simple: in the first part the choir sang psalms while the congregation sang a refrain after every verse (this enabled full participation in a world where books were not available). These psalms were carefully chosen for their suitability, the accent being on praise and thanksgiving. After each psalm there was a silence and then a prayer, summing up the psalm. At evening this service was preceded with the lighting of the lamps: starting with a darkened church, they gradually lit the lamps, while singing the praise of Christ as the light of the world. When all the psalmody was over, they went straight into the second part of the service, petition and intercession. Prayers were offered in the form of a litany, which, like the psalms, usually provided a repeated refrain for the congregation to sing.

If people could not get to church, they prayed where they were, uniting themselves with the prayers offered by the gathered faithful in church. This is what was meant first and foremost when they talked of Christian prayer: prayer that was rooted in the community, and in the words of the Scriptures, well-loved prayer that had grown up through repeated praying by many generations. Thus the natural home of prayer was in the gathered Body of Christ, but this prayer was designed so that even when Christians were alone it was as if they were praying with others. Our picture of praying huddled in some private place, or trying to "turn on" great "devotion", is not so much historically unfounded as spiritually inappropriate. Secluded personal prayer is a form of "advanced" praying that should be based upon experience first of all of the daily worship of the Church, the daily hours of prayer in Christ to God.

This tradition of Christian prayer in community lasted a very long time and after a while communal or common prayer began to lose its fresh and popular character for a number of social, political and economic reasons.

One tell-tale sign of this change emerged by the ninth century when the daily services in the West were beginning to be taken over entirely by the clergy. By the fourteenth century the services were completely transformed. The daily services still took place in parish churches, but were sung by the clerics entirely in Latin, which most worshippers could not understand. People came in to share in the worship but because of the language barrier they would say their own prayers while the service continued around them. In addition, the meaning behind the services had altered: originally they had been an act of praise offered by the whole people of God, in order to mark the passage of the hours; by this point, they had become something different, a quota of words which the clergy had by Church law to "get through". This, combined with a fall in attendance due to the decreasing popularity of these services meant that the clergy began to read the words (now merely an onerous duty) in private, rather than singing them with the body of believers in church in a liturgical celebration. The Church's liturgy was rapidly drying up, leaving Christians with little alternative but to try and do what they could on their own. So there grew up that "private prayer", which we now assume to be the norm, but which was, in reality, a compensation for having lost the "proper prayer" of the Church. Such prayer was and is a second-best, make-do affair.

Christians coped with this liturgical "drought" in various ways. Some found their sustenance in "meditation" or silent prayer. Such prayer has always had an important place alongside common Christian prayer from the time of

12

the New Testament and the Church Fathers onwards, but unlike common prayer it was not the norm and was not to be sought for. Rather, for those to whom it came naturally, it was seen as a gift. For this reason, St Benedict makes no mention of silent prayer in his Rule for monks, only that if an urge for solitary prayer is felt, it should be welcomed but that the time in such prayer should be brief. One of the sole benefits of this unfortunate development away from common prayer to silent and solitary prayer was the systematic pursuit of interior prayer as a direct route to God in imitation of the hermits, anchorites of solitaries who, like the Lady Julian of Norwich, became teachers and examples in a highly specialised vocation to holiness.

Another way in which people adapted to the loss of their well-tried and popular rhythm of prayer in church was to keep it going, in simplified ways, in the folk tradition. An outstanding example of this is the popularity, among modern Christians, of the ever-popular Office of Compline. Other forms of prayer strayed further from the liturgy until they became free-standing forms of popular "piety" such as the Angelus or the Rosary (in origin a simple way of saying the Psalter). These devotions largely lost their sense of being the worship of the Church, congregational worship full of a sense of the Body of Christ. They became individual acts of piety, something that early Christians would have thought sad, lonely, and lacking that strong sense of the Body of Christ which flavours all descriptions of prayer in the early years.

From about 1800 to 1960 the whole tradition of daily prayer as it was found in the various churches went through a particularly difficult period. In Roman Catholicism it was more or less lost to all but the clergy, while in Anglicanism it very nearly disappeared before experiencing a revival during the Oxford Movement.

The situation we are left with today is one in which we have ended up with a strange "personal" approach to prayer, where we assume it is something to be done in private, that we have to have a deep personal experience if

13

it is worthwhile, and that to pray you have to be a particularly holy person. The result is that many people do not pray, or if they do, they find it extremely difficult and unrewarding. Similarly, many clergy are becoming less and less satisfied by the "Office" provided for private recitation. *The Alternative Service Book 1980* made only textual adjustments to the daily services of the Book of Common Prayer, and did not address the question of the suitability of the form or content.

There were and are, however, some exceptions to this rather sad history. The Book of Common Prayer provided that the bell should toll to call parishioners to church daily for Matins and Evensong. This persisted in many town churches and, although difficult to sustain, significant proportions of country churches held these services on most days of the week, and people did attend, sometimes in large numbers. When services were not held, it was very common for the priest to say the Offices with his household. Meanwhile, in the cathedrals there has been an unrivalled tradition of daily Choral Evensong (and, until recently, Choral Matins as well) as was the tradition in the early centuries. Even in the early 1990s interesting experiments have been going on in the United States, and in France and other European countries. There are now parishes where a corporate service of worship takes place twice a day, and, contrary to what might have been supposed, this is becoming popular in more and more Christian communities.

Much has been discovered about the daily prayer of the Church: that it is essentially corporate; involves music, movement, the visual and the sensory, and belongs to the whole people of God. So much is happening now in different places, that the time seems ripe for a move forward in the Church of England. It is because of this that *Celebrating Common Prayer* has been produced, gathering together the fruits of widespread experience in order to make available a rich and adaptable source of material, in the conviction that the time is now ripe for a recovery of the essential spirit (without slavish imitation) of the ancient Christian hours of prayer. Perhaps the most important parts of the book are the two forms of Office, both of which are intended for daily liturgical use in parishes and Christian communities, and are also capable of being prayed in private.

The main form is rich and varied, and capable of meeting the needs both of worshipping groups and individuals who normally have no opportunity to pray together with others. For the latter the richness of the provision is particularly helpful in a situation where the ASB is rather lean.

The "Simple Celebration" form arises out of a successful experiment in a northern town parish over several years, and is already being used in many other parts of the country. The verdict of those who have used this form and the main form is unanimous: people find that in this way they can pray. Not only is it historical, it is natural to pray by saying or singing the psalms and prayers of the Church, and with a tremendous sense of *belonging*, a sense of praying with Christians everywhere, whether praying as a group or praying alone. For we, being many, are one Body, and it is in the Body that we discover what it means to pray. In the Body we find Christ, and so our prayer is no longer a private struggle, but becomes Christ praying in us. We are rediscovering the experience of the apostles, the experience of belonging together within the living mystery of Christ's resurrection. This is something many Christians have lost sight of, and it lies at the heart of the Gospel. Reading about the history of prayer can enable us to rediscover our lost inheritance but it is only through action that a return can be made to true Christian prayer.

2 ◆ Using the Bible in daily prayer

MARTIN KITCHEN

1. Using the Bible Today

How is it possible to "use" a text? For Christian people, the Bible is, in some sense, "the Word of God", and it underlies, sustains and exercises some authority over the life of the Church. As such it should be heard, responded to, and cherished. Some would say that it is inappropriate to think of "using" it; others would claim that it is only when we enter into a lively relationship with the text and "use" it to develop the life and thought of the Church that we can become aware of its special character.

Before we go on to think about how the Bible might be used, we need to consider what it is. The word "Bible" is a slippery term, because people who employ it mean different things by it. Roman Catholics have a larger Bible than Protestants, and Evangelicals have one which hovers somewhere between the two. We have to acknowledge that part of our scriptures come to us from Judaism, but we still have to recognise that the Hebrew Bible differs from the Greek in what it contains. Nevertheless, a Bible of some kind has been in use since the formation of the Church two millennia ago. Since the Reformation of the Western Church in the sixteenth century (nearly half a millennium ago!) it has been possible to study it without the constraints of dogmatic theology. And in the past two centuries, critical study of its texts, its theology and its emphases has led to the conclusion that the idea of "using" earlier traditions, both written and oral, is very ancient indeed. Earlier editors and compilers selected and omitted texts to suit their own purposes. The writers of the Gospels made use of earlier traditions, both written and oral; and the writer of the Epistle to the Ephesians made use of the Epistle to the Colossians. Similarly, the Bible always has been and continues to be "used" by all Christian communities and groups.

One way of "using" it is to turn to it in order to learn

about God, about Christian doctrine, and about how to live
life "in the Spirit". Another way is to read it in the attempt
to discover the history of the Jewish people, to learn what
Jesus said and did, to know what happened to the early
Christians, and therefore to have an idea of how the life of
the Church should, perhaps, be ordered today. Yet another
way of "using" the Bible is to dig into it for texts to prove
a point in an argument, or to persuade someone that one's
own view of Christian life is closest to what God intends or
intended. We must also acknowledge that the Bible has
been – and still is – used by some to justify war against
"ungodly people", oppression of whole nations, and forms
of punishment which, were they not apparently warranted
in "Scripture", would be seen to be against every canon of
charitable and righteous behaviour.

Clearly, some of these uses of the Bible are more justifiable than others. One principal use of the Bible, however,
is in the worship of God. Indeed, it is so common now to
see the Bible being put to all sorts of uses, justifiable and
unjustifiable, that it is easy to forget that the first use of
the Bible was to assist Jewish and Christian people in their
worship of God.

The community of people would come together, and a
passage of Scripture would be read for the people to hear.
The passage would frequently be about what God had done
for the people's "salvation", or ultimate wellbeing. The
expectation was that God was speaking in the text, and that
the people were privileged to hear God's Word addressing
them. In the days of the earliest Christians, as well as reading texts from the Jewish scriptures (which had already
been translated two centuries before the birth of Christ into
the common language of the Mediterranean world, which
was Greek), letters from other leaders and communities
would also be read. The focus was still upon what God had
done and what God required, loving one another, and caring for their neighbours, but this would remind the people
of God's particular care for them and of the response due
from them to God in worship. As time went on, stories

circulated about the life of Jesus, and these were gradually collected into written documents, which we have come to call "gospels", because they were versions of the one "gospel" (or "good news") of God's reign which was begun in the earthly life and ministry of Jesus.

2. Prayer – Common and Biblical

The form of daily prayer (or "Daily Office") in the Church focuses the community's attention upon those texts which are foundational to its life. Other writers in this volume are concentrating upon the Lectionary and the use of the Psalms in *Celebrating Common Prayer*. Our concern is the general "feel" of the Office as it provides the context for the reading of scripture and the singing of psalms.

In the sixteenth century, when Archbishop Thomas Cranmer was planning worship for the reformed Church of England, he took as the basis for the service of Morning and Evening Prayer the Offices of the medieval Church, and adapted them so that they could become vehicles for the reading and hearing of the Bible. One of the main purposes of Daily Prayer was to provide a series of opportunities for the Christian community to read the Bible. When the monks of the earlier centuries retreated from the snares (as they perceived them) of their contemporary world, they expected to meet with God. As they developed communities, they developed a pattern of worship which was based upon singing the Psalms and reading the Scriptures. It is this tradition that informed the development of the Office in the Church at large, and which Cranmer saw as the key to having the Bible read in parish churches across the nation, so that the people could hear and understand it.

Some might ask, "Why develop a liturgy for reading the Bible? Can it not be read without introduction or embellishment? Does the Spirit of God need to be couched in acceptable forms to be able to speak to the ear of the Church?" Well, of course, the Spirit "needs" no such things; the point is that the Bible is always heard within a context, and that

context is the worship of God's people. The medieval Offices
broke up the day into units, when monks would work,
sleep, pray or study. It also broke up the text of Scripture
into manageable portions, so that there developed a pace,
or rhythm, of life together. So, both the text of the Bible
and the whole day were divided into sections which allowed
for and encouraged the offering of the whole of life in worship to God.

Naturally, because the reading of the Bible was an act of
worship, other elements of worship were included in the
service. There were introductory prayers, ascriptions of
praise, responses to the reading, songs and hymns – from
the Bible and elsewhere – collects (prayers which "collected
together" the desires of the whole congregation), versicles
and responses, acclamations, and so on. By reading through
any part of the liturgy in *Celebrating Common Prayer* the
reader will see many passages of Scripture being used in this
way and the use of a concordance will make it easier to find
these references in the text of a Bible.

Some Christians are very good at quoting the Bible from
memory. There are preachers and leaders who specialise
in this approach to encouraging Christian discipleship, and
there are many Christian people who like to find texts
which seem to apply to all facets of their life. The danger of
this, of course, is that any such quotation takes the passage
of Scripture "out of context", and therefore makes it mean
something which is far removed from the setting it enjoyed
in a foreign language and a different culture nearly two
thousand years ago. Examples of quotation (correctly used)
in the course of the Office are, of course, the many occasions
when versicles and responses are said, such as "O Lord,
open our lips", with the response, "And our mouth
shall proclaim your praise". In addition, refrains are used
before and after psalms and canticles – and the Canticles
themselves are passages of Scripture which lend themselves to singing as an expression of the community's
worship.

Another way of using the Bible which is related to, but

not the same as, quotation is allusion. This is a more subtle and "impressionistic" approach to the text, which allows words and phrases to resonate (literally, "to sound again") at various levels of meaning in the minds of speakers and readers, writers and hearers. It is in this way that liturgical texts best recall the words of the Bible, and there are many examples of this in *Celebrating Common Prayer*. For example, the acclamations which constitute an option in the Preparation are full of biblical allusions to the creation of humankind in God's image, the coming into the world of the Word made flesh, God's redemption of the world in Christ, and the various titles which are given to God and to Christ.

An interesting and rewarding spiritual exercise might be to go through the text of any of the orders of service printed in *Celebrating Common Prayer* and try to work out – perhaps with the aid of a concordance – where a particular word, phrase or passage might come from in the Bible. Such a mental awareness of the connection between the text of the Scriptures and the text of the liturgy can enhance the degree to which, as worshippers, we may find the "text" of our own lives paralleled before us, and so find ourselves nourished by the Word of God.

3. Worship and the Bible Today

The observation that there is value in thinking and learning about what we are doing as we worship reminds us that worship is not a mindless activity, any more than faith is blind to the interests of the intellect. The word "Bible" means "books" – a collection – and the plural, *ta biblia*, itself implies variety. A variety of approaches to and uses of the Bible is therefore appropriate. We may listen with a view to picking up and cherishing a phrase or sentence upon which we will meditate during the day. We may hope for a particular note of encouragement about God's faithfulness when our spirits are low. We may listen and ask critical questions about the history the Bible purports to tell, noting inconsistencies, for example, in the resurrection narratives,

or we may question the morality of some of God's com-
mands (like the one to strike dead all the enemies of the
people of Israel).

Questions like these – and many others – have been put
to the text of the Bible increasingly over the past two centuries. Scholars and other readers have begun to acknowledge that the text of the Bible, just like any other text,
is written in a language which is different from our own.
Translation is not without its difficulties in the case of any
text, but when the text is also from an ancient culture there
are additional problems to be faced, and these are all the
more pressing when the text has religious significance for a
vast number of people.

To say that the Bible is of such significance in worship is
not, of course, to say that the Bible deserves to be wor-
shipped or to be read uncritically. There are obvious problems associated with such an approach. The first is the
problem of the different view of the world which we have
today. There are now many theories to account for the
creation of the world; illness is not attributed to God's displeasure; we understand much about the nature of things
that exist. Secondly, there is the question of historical
reliability. Some of the stories in the Bible are difficult to
reconcile. The four stories we have of the resurrection of
Jesus, for example, cannot be put together in one narrative,
and there are many today who find it hard to see how the
Jesus of the fourth Gospel – who knows his divine origin –
can equate with the Jesus of the first three Gospels, who
speaks and acts in quite a different tone, dismissing any
attempt to rank him above his fellows. Thirdly, there is the
problem of morality. We struggle with the idea that it is
God's will for nations to be wiped out for the sake of the
military success of one particular people. We also understand our sexuality rather differently today; we know that
the two sexes have an equal role in the procreation of children (one of the issues that this Office book takes seriously
is that of inclusive language) and that there are varieties
of sexual orientation which are not simply the result of

21

disobedience to God. Fourthly, and this is perhaps the most significant difference, there is the problem of God. Unlike our forebears, who used the concept of God to explain the world and history, and the destiny of nations and individuals, we now need to integrate faith with the scientific and historical causes of events, and with that which we understand of human psychology and decision-making.

The questions which arise in the mind of the modern critical reader are therefore not to be dismissed as inappropriate for Christian disciples, but might rather cause us to wonder what it is about this God who so captivated the imagination of a nation; or how would we today give expression to the sense of meaning which our faith provides; or how might we apply Christian categories of thought to the very documents which provide a basis for Christian being; and how do we hold together those complex and often contradictory elements within our holy scriptures. Seeking the answers to these questions can provide us with material for progressing in faith and love for God and for our neighbours.

Many of these issues come to the fore especially in the context of the Midday Office in *Celebrating Common Prayer*, since readings additional to the Lectionary have been selected to provide material for reflection upon a set of concerns which is very modern and, therefore, far removed from the concerns of the world which gave birth to the books of the Bible. Nevertheless we have attempted to strike a balance between, on the one hand, a flat reading of the Bible, which assumes that there are no problems of a cultural gap between the earlier generations of Jews and Christians and ourselves, and a set of assumptions which would assume that the gap was too great to bridge.

Part of the pleasure of going to the theatre is taking in all the theatrical trappings which we see around the foyer. Within an order for a Daily Office, the Bible has a function which is, in some sense, like those pictures which form the context within which we see a play produced. The main texts are those of the Bible and of the liturgy itself which

forms the all-important context in which it is read. However, we can see that there is also a sense in which the text
of the Bible surrounds itself, in the words of the liturgy, and
as we say the Office we are caught up in the whole drama
of God's involvement in human living.

4. Celebrating Common Prayer

Much contemporary thinking is concerned with the significance of texts – indeed, some modern philosophers question
whether anything exists outside writing and beyond texts.
Here is not the place to discuss this issue and its relation to
Christian worship in any detail, but we might hold on to
the image of our life – together and as individuals – as
"text"; for, when we think about our lives and tell their
story (or stories), we create a "text". That text includes the
narration of events in our life that include our experience
of ourselves, of other people, of the world, and of God.
Worship provides us with the opportunity to set that "text"
alongside the sacred text(s) of our faith, so that we may
recognise in both the presence of God. To do this is to do a
number of things. First, it is to acknowledge that our life is
lived in dependence upon and in relationship with God and
other people. Second, it is to perceive that such an acknowledgment calls for celebration, while at the same time providing the words and forms for the celebration to take place.
Third, it is to accept the responsibility which necessarily
goes hand in hand with the acknowledgment of God, and
to resolve to live in such a way that the worship and service
of God become the priority of our living.

Praying the Daily Office involves dividing up the text of
the Bible so that it can be read and savoured in appropri-
ately-sized portions. What the Office also does is to divide
up the hours of the day, the days of the week and the weeks
of the year, so that each portion of it may be made into an
offering to God. This has the effect of making the whole of
time holy.

The compilers of *Celebrating Common Prayer* hope that it
will live up to its title, for its choice was deliberate. Christian

people are used to "celebrating" the Eucharist, and the language of "celebration" is widespread in the context of the sacraments. However, the Office is "celebrated" too. The reason for this is that Christian people are invited to *enjoy* their relationship with God, for there is in it something to celebrate. People who believe in God acknowledge the mystery that is at the heart of reality, recognise that mystery as personal, and address that mystery as God. The many-faceted witness of the various stories, reflections, poems and epistles in the Bible assure us that God's being, however mysterious, is expressed in relationship with the creation and with his creatures who are made capable of responding in love and devotion.

In Christ and by God's Spirit we are invited to share in God's being, to share in whatever is life-giving, in whatever brings about reconciliation between people and nations, and to know that whatever speaks of forgiveness is of God. Prayer that is "common" arises from an awareness that people belong together, not least when they stand together before God. There is much to celebrate in this belief, and it is the Bible that records for us the experience of men and women across the ages who have discovered that to be so. As we meditate upon the Scriptures, we stand, like Moses, upon holy ground and we may hear the voice of God calling us with good news for ourselves and for our neighbour.

3 ◆ The spirituality of the daily office

JOHN MICHAEL MOUNTNEY

It is worth asking the question: for whose benefit is the liturgy of the Church designed and performed? A careful study of Anglican worship today reveals a trend begun in the dawn of liturgical renewal, that required that the worshipper should participate more fully in the liturgy; that people should understand what is being said and done; and that the style of worship should be of a kind to which ordinary people can relate. Obviously, one cannot quarrel with this, but the trend seems to have brought a ghost to the banquet, and the ghost is one which has made contemporary worship extremely people-centred. There is, for instance, the rich, ritualistic sung Eucharist, sometimes sought out by those who go with the intention of receiving rather than giving. In terms of people-centred worship we might call this the liturgy of passivity. Then there is the Sunday service where teaching becomes the driving element (the didactic liturgy), and there are services which people attend in order to leave behind the strains of everyday living, and to experience the release of all that is pent-up and frustrated (the therapeutic liturgy). There again, we shall find a wide and sophisticated provision for children and young people (the liturgy of nurture), and in a large majority of cases even Baptism services are timed and tailored to the individual family (the liturgy of childbirth). We can look further and discover a host of prayer meetings and house groups and vigils for special occasions and causes (the liturgy of need), and one ought not to omit the special provision of worship from the Book of Common Prayer (the liturgy of concession). We all, no doubt, go to church with one or more of those expectations of the liturgy, and all those elements cry out to be satisfied to a greater or lesser degree in each of us, but there is a danger. All the requirements listed above suggest a view of worship that is essentially *self*-centred.

Study of the Daily Office, however, leads us to another conclusion, that Morning and Evening Prayer are supremely the liturgy of worshipping, and are therefore God-centred. And that startling discovery may go some way to explain why Morning and Evening Prayer are such unpopular services in these times, both on Sundays, and as the vital, if small part of a parish's life of daily prayer. The Daily Office makes no concessions to anyone, because it is not a service for "consumers", it is a service *for God* (the liturgy of God).

Any examination of its forms instantly make this clear, and a balanced study will mean travelling back before 1662 or 1549, and beyond the known territories of Anglicanism. What emerges is a liturgy that is predominantly one of praise to God, because we find psalmody, canticles and scriptural responsories in abundance, and all designed to be sung, not muttered. And we find intercession occupying a more central position than is sometimes allowed for in the liturgies at our disposal. Moreover, the great weight laid on Scripture reading in the Office we find a rather modern idea, and somewhat out of tune with the earlier tradition of the Office, because it has to be said that the principle of meting out long didactic Bible readings at Morning and Evening Prayer was a characteristic preoccupation of the Reformation period. It can no longer be an issue now that we can all buy, read, mark and learn the Bible as much as we like, and with more profit, in the quiet of our own homes.

The Daily Office is the form of prayer that has been offered to God daily in the Church for many, many centuries, which is why it can claim to be *the* prayer of *the* Church. It is objective in ethos, leading us away from ourselves, and formal in its structure, that is to say, having its set form, which we tamper with at our peril. That it is a formal kind of worship is not to say that it cannot be celebrated intimately by two or three gathered together in a small corner of a large church, which is why some bishops today are urging the provision of at least one act of worship in every rural church on Sundays, however lightly attended, and why in every parish church (or one in a group) Morning and Evening Prayer need to be celebrated daily. Thus the whole Church is present when just a few meet for this liturgy. To suggest that it is not worth having a service because so few come is to invert the whole understanding of the worship of God, and speaks again of a people-centred approach to worship.

We ought now to consider that the Daily Office is also known as the liturgy of time. All other services, including the Eucharist and Confirmation, can be administered at any time of the day or night. Morning Prayer emphatically cannot be said in the evening. The morning and evening are crucial times of day for the human being re-awakening to consciousness, and resting after a day's work. Life is governed by its rhythms, the rhythms within, the rhythms of passing day, the rhythms of the universe and the created order. We are rhythmic creatures and we live in a rhythmic sequence of time, not only the daily and weekly ones, but also those of birth and infancy leading to childhood, to adolescence, maturity, old age and death. The Church, too, has her rhythms. Time is crucial to the unfolding of the mysteries of the faith, and we can only absorb their meaning with time. So, the birth of Jesus speaks of the Incarnation, and his death of the Atonement. Morning Prayer speaks of resurrection, and Midday Prayer of death on the cross; Evening Prayer of rest, and darkness and judgment, lightened by Christ the light of the world. So it is no surprise to discover that the Daily Office has a simple origin in public prayer at morning and evening, sometimes called the Cathedral tradition.

Celebrating Common Prayer leaves us in no doubt that the Daily Office is the liturgy of time. We are offered Morning and Evening Prayer, as you would expect, but also Midday Prayer and Night Prayer (Compline). There are many who find the four Hour system congenial, but most will find

Morning and Evening Prayer quite sufficient. Apart from the obvious question of the timing of these Hours, in what other way do they speak of time? We shall often find in the cycle of psalms references appropriate to the time of day, as we shall in the collects. People either rejoice in or complain at innovations in the liturgy, but in reality there is nothing new under the sun, and the character of all modern liturgical revision has been to ransack the storehouses of the tradition, and to bring out what is old and now made new. Inevitably people will detect "innovations" in *Celebrating Common Prayer*. One such is the new Preparation section; out goes the penitential section, though one can always be included if desired, but the one offered at Night Prayer really says it all. Instead we have a call to worship in the usual way with opening responses and the Glory to the Father with Alleluia, or instead, an acclamatory prayer clearly acknowledging the time of day. Both of these are reinforced by the responses to that call in the Opening Canticle and the Opening Prayer. In Midday Prayer we find the concerns of the working day expressed in the themes offered. At Evening Prayer an alternative Preparation gives us an opportunity to use the ancient but simple and very powerful ceremony of the lighting of the lamps in the gathering darkness (which has its roots in the Jewish domestic liturgy) that includes the *Phos Hilaron*, "Hail, Gladdening Light", found in one or other form in most hymnbooks, followed by the Evening Psalm.

At Night Prayer the traditional night hymn, "Before the Ending of the Day", is sung and psalmody chosen for its references to night and sleep, as is the Gospel Canticle (the *Nunc Dimittis*), its refrain and other responses. There is a night blessing. On the whole there is nothing in the above that is at variance with the spirit of the versions of the Daily Office that we already have, but it is in its presentation and wide choices of material that *Celebrating Common Prayer* is enabled to make clearer emphases within a more subtle structure. We ought not to overlook that other inescapable unit of time, the week. So, as in the past, there is provision to say the collect of the week (usually the preceding Sunday) at least at Morning and Evening Prayer each day. This is a great strength.

But it is something much more fundamental to the content of *Celebrating Common Prayer* that makes this new version stand apart from the others. In a way never possible with *The Book of Common Prayer* or *The Alternative Service Book 1980* we are enabled to celebrate that other dimension of time which is always latent in the Daily Office, the unfolding of the mysteries of the faith that the calendar of the Church has prepared over the centuries. Accordingly, each day of the week in *Celebrating Common Prayer* has been allotted a seasonal theme, explained in more detail elsewhere, but to give an example, Sundays will always have the theme of resurrection, and Mondays the Spirit, and so on. Seven has always been a significant number in Scripture, but there is something eschatological about the concept of the seven daily themes chosen for this version of the Office entirely appropriate to the liturgy of time. The Christian age is the last age, a sort of perpetual Saturday, in which we await the eighth new and glorious age, the age of our own resurrection and glory and of Christ's second coming (the liturgy of expectation). So each week we make our way through the mysteries of the faith, Incarnation at Christmas, the revelation of Epiphany, the cross in Lent and Passiontide, resurrection at Easter, followed by Pentecost and the Spirit, the Kingdom season and the anticipation of that kingdom in Advent. During those seasons the Office allows those themes to develop in the material offered; in canticles, responsories and refrains to the canticles, as well as collects. Even the psalms have been chosen to make the appropriate connections. In the "green" season, on the other hand, whilst never losing sight of these themes as we pray through the week, they are never allowed to dominate. Of course, in the lectionary schemes of the Church of England, the Scripture readings have borne the weight of unfolding the mysteries of the faith. The new arrangement allows for a more poetic rather than didactic approach, and this in turn brings into play parts of Scripture not at first obviously connected with a given mystery, and endows them with new and rich significance.

But the action of time upon the mysteries of the faith does not stop with the daily themes. In a way unprecedented the new Office provides us with a wealth of material for the celebration of the saints of the Church. The thrust of the Reformation was admittedly away from the cult of the saints, for all sorts of reasons, some good. But we ignore the saints at our peril; neither the BCP nor the ASB calendars allow us to forget them, and both books make excellent provision at the Eucharist, if less in the Office. Assuredly, we shall celebrate the existence of the saints and their life and witness, to the glory of God and to our profit. And the reason is simple. It has already been stated that we are engaged in the prayer of the Church, and that must include the whole Church, not just that here on earth. The saints in heaven have the specific task of worshipping God incessantly, and praying for the rest of us. If anyone knows how to celebrate the Daily Office, it is the saints, and theirs is the twenty-four Hour version! It is an understanding of the Office of this sort that enables John McQuarrie (*Paths in Spirituality*, London: SCM, 1972. pp104–5), to assert that praying the Daily Office is to be caught up in the divine order, a serene and stable order, an order of justice and peace that one might with justification call the Kingdom of God itself; and Paul Bradshaw (*The Identity of Anglican Worship*, ed. Stevenson and Spinks, London: Mowbray, 1991. p69f), to state that we are doing what God created us most specially to do, to worship him as a royal priesthood. If heaven should ever seem remote and unattainable, then at least the recitation of the Daily Office avails us of it in some small measure. Anyone who has listened to Evensong being sung by a cathedral choir ought also to have some idea about the point being made. It is in heaven that we find the saints, but at the same time they are alongside us in prayer and praise. It has always been possible to celebrate a saint's day in the Office with a collect and a well-chosen hymn, whilst books of non-canonical readings are readily available to supplement the usual lessons with something of their glory and encouragement for us. But in *Celebrating Common Prayer* fitting canticles and responsories are also supplied which enable us within the framework of time to transcend our time and space and to be at one with their celebration above. We should learn to love the saints a little and take heart from what they are doing for us; then they will cease to seem remote from us or irrelevant and our spirituality will have been deepened.

But there is more to be said about time, or should one say timing? It seems extraordinary to be insisting on the Daily Office as the liturgy of time, without allowing time to work to advantage for its proper celebration. Most of us live action-packed lives, and we all suffer from the resulting stress. We are not finding time in our lives to "stand and stare". We need space, and time for space, and so does the celebration of the liturgy of time. The temptation to "get it over and done with" has to be resisted strongly, and the busier we are the greater the effort needed to give it time; not time to prolong things unnecessarily (already we are confronted with a formidable array of words), but time to allow the liturgy "to breathe". All those words will not make a lot of sense unless due time is allowed for those words and the silences in between them. There are obvious places for silences in the rite. A proper pause is needed at the break in the psalm and canticle verses, indicated by the asterisk; before collects, especially if one is used at the end of a psalm. The psalm collect has two uses; the first is that it prevents us from forgetting that a psalm is prayer as well as praise, and the second that it is a very efficient disc-brake when the temptation to take the psalmody at a gallop is overwhelming. A silence is appropriate after the readings, too. There will also be times when the Intercession section will benefit from a minimum of words and a maximum of silence. The use of words in intercession should never be didactic, telling people – and often God – what to do or what they already know, but should aim to set people free to pray as the Spirit leads with a minimum of prompting.

It is in the silences that God can finally speak; they are the moments of the truest prayer. Robert Llewelyn has described the words of prayer as the banks between which the silent river of prayer flows (*Doorway to Silence*, London: Darton, Longman & Todd, 1986. p20). But it will not flow if due regard is not paid to the sense of rhythm and order that the liturgy must be allowed to engender. In sensitive hands the Office can be a verbal choreography of solemn and stately rhythms and in that lies its prayerful beauty. If it should seem that we are now coming to a more contemplative understanding of the Office, then so be it; this is nothing new. It is certainly essential to anticipate that dimension for it is assuredly present, and it is legitimate to partake in the Office in a passive way in certain circumstances (the liturgy of contemplation). Because all prayer finally requires that moment of surrender that is contemplation, the Office has the potential to trigger this if it is celebrated sensitively; all the great contemplatives will have served a substantial apprenticeship in the Daily Office.

I have already made some remarks about the choice of psalms, but something needs to be said about the function they fulfil. They are the chief medium by which the praise of God is made, they are far more ancient than any hymn, and they are refreshingly honest. Like the *News of the World*, all human life is there! They unfailingly speak to our condition, whether we find ourselves "in the pit" or hating "with a perfect hatred". The Psalms give us permission to feel angry and violent, even murderous in the presence of God because Christ himself is present in the Psalms. By helping us to face up to the thoughts we would prefer not to have, saying the Psalms can absolve us from our darkest moods. By this means the Psalms can transport us away from our sloughs, and empower us to sing to the Lord a new song. Hymns, by contrast, rarely allow us to start where we really are. To match their lofty sentiments we need to have been in the "A" team for a long time. For this reason the urge to replace psalms with hymns needs to be resisted.

Spirituality will develop and mature immeasurably when ordinary people are allowed to get to grips with the Psalms. It is worth spending time and effort getting people to say or sing them prayerfully and effectively. Neither need be difficult or complicated.

The sense of the presence of Christ in the Psalms was so overpowering to the Church Fathers that they called their writer the Prophet. Moreover, a spirituality that does not reckon with the Psalms is cut off both from our Anglican and Jewish roots, and from Scripture itself, so it is surprising (and tragic) that they are absent from so much that is offered as the Church's worship. Frequently, worship that attempts to meet our need fails, or at least leaves us in the misery we hoped to escape. This takes us back to my original question, to whom is worship directed? Following an almost forgotten tradition *Celebrating Common Prayer* offers us another treasure in its arrangement of psalmody; the so-called Alleluia or *Laudate* psalms at Morning Prayer. Those Hebrew and Latin words mean "Praise the Lord", which is the opening line of Psalms 117 and 146–150. After allowing for Psalm 147 to be divided that provides one psalm of praise to round off morning psalmody for each day of the week. This gives the morning's psalmody a clear pattern; first the Opening Canticle, usually a psalm chosen for its invitation to praise God, then, after the Opening Prayer a psalm chosen for its morning associations, next an Old Testament Canticle chosen for the theme of the day (e.g. Advent) and finally the *Laudate* psalm with its clear and resounding alleluias. This will give the Office a greater sense of purpose than the old arrangements where psalmody was chosen at random, and in some cases could seem quite inappropriate. Mention of the Old Testament Canticle calls for further comment. This is an extension of the tradition, barely retained in the BCP and more obviously present in the ASB, that allows us to sing other scriptural passages of importance and beauty, although they have a very different structure and rhythm. At Evening Prayer this idea has been extended to include a New Testament Canticle for the same reason. Partly because of the special character of the canticles they are given refrains, which help to draw out their theme, and allow them to stand in their own space.

At this point some may question the amount of repetition that is found in the Office. It has been known for a long time that repeated prayer has great value. The mantras of the East bear this out. The repetition of prayers or phrases from Scripture does two things. Firstly, a prayer that can be said by heart enables us to concentrate on the heart, and the conscious processes of reading or following can give place to the unconscious ones. Secondly, the more often a phrase is said the more deeply it can penetrate our hearts. Much modern liturgy tends to be linear in its movement; we are led from a beginning to an end, by which time it is hoped that we have in some measure been edified. But the Office is unashamedly cyclic; it does churn round, and it is not a sin to be bored by it at times. Repetition needs to be understood and accepted as a valid method of prayer, because the circumstances of night following day and the givenness of Scripture require it to be so. The worship of Taizé has also taught us much about the value of repetition. It is a pity that so many in their oriental search did not stop to find the mantras of the West, like "Lord have mercy" or "Glory be to the Father". The temptation to tailor liturgy only to the conscious mind is another modern "ghost".

Before we leave the subject of canticles a few words need to be said about the Gospel Canticles; the *Benedictus, Magnificat* and *Nunc Dimittis*. Though not "compulsory" in either the BCP or the ASB it is normal to have them, for each has a double function. First, they provide a kind of climax (especially if sung) to the first part of the liturgy; the prophetic nature of the psalmody and Scripture readings resolve in a short, poetic "Gospel Celebration", before the liturgy turns to the business of intercession, its second main task. Secondly, the Gospel Canticles are themselves a summation of the Gospel message, and if one did not have time to say the whole Office, repetition of the Gospel Canticles would be a complete act of worship.

The question of intercession has been mentioned and must now be addressed. The Kyries may be used in any of their forms, and stand more firmly in the Church's tradition of intercession than of penitence, and the fixed, short litany has given way to the choice of the many available appropriate to the occasion. The collect remains in its task of collecting our individual prayers together (and extempore biddings are encouraged) in a concluding formula. The main change here is the placing of the Lord's Prayer afterwards to give the liturgy a strong ending, where often the work of intercession has started strongly with the set prayers but then straggled into a ragbag at the end.

In the notes for the use of the Office there is a suggestion that the Conclusion might include the words, "The Lord be with you", although they are not printed out. It was Peter Damian ("The Book of the Lord be with you" in *Selected Writings in the Spiritual Life*, trans. Patricia McNulty, London: Faber & Faber, 1959. p53) who told his monks that they should always use that form in their recitation of the Office, for the very reason that there was no one else with them in their hut, a situation often paralleled by a priest saying the Office today. To say those words is to remind us of the rest of the Church Militant here on earth and it is vital not to lose that dimension, just as it is vital not to lose that of the Heavenly Church, and if the Office had been used more in the past it might not have seemed such a lonely affair. But talk of conclusions must bring this chapter to its end as well.

I began by pointing out certain movements in Anglican worship today. It needs to be emphasised that the Daily Office has given Anglicanism its unique character of worship and spirituality. Much of *The Book of Common Prayer* is dedicated to its celebration, and in less eucharistically-centred and family service-centred days it was the heart and soul of the weekly worship for generations of Anglicans, to the point where it became the envy of Roman Catholic and Free Churchman alike. As Martin Thornton pointed out (in *English Spirituality*, London: SPCK, 1992. pp262, 270), its strengths lay in its power to create a complete, comprehensive system of prayer and spirituality, which made it acceptable to all and alienated none, whilst taking cognisance of the human state in all its forms. Whether celebrated silently and singly in a country church or rendered exquisitely in "places where they sing", it has spoken of the order and serenity of the Kingdom of Heaven on earth, of the worship of God at its profoundest. Consequently, it has been spiritually nourishing in the richest of ways. Above all, it celebrated itself, it "carried you", and required no brain-racking on the part of the officiant (or overhead projections). It was the Church's prayer, and as such Christ himself was found to be praying in it, inspired, as is all prayer, by the Spirit. It has been all those things, and in reality must still be. Here we can leave behind the bustle of daily life and enter into the quietness of the Church's prayer. That such a jewel (the Crown Jewels, really) should have been allowed to gather dust and tarnish in recent times speaks of a need to look once more for a treasure lost and rejoice at its being found.

This is not, however, a call to some mythical "good old days" or to pitch the Eucharist from its present and central place in the Church so hard won. But it is a call to roll the tradition forward, at once traditional and renewed, a jewel re-set and freshly polished to a new and richer glory. But man is not saved by paper and print, or even rubrics alone, as all modern liturgical revision has shown. There has to be a new spirit, and a new or reawakened spirituality. Much hard and imaginative work has gone into the creation of *Celebrating Common Prayer*, and it is this writer's most earnest hope that that spirituality will be lovingly and widely rediscovered by the daily use of this volume.

4 ◆ Praying the Psalms

David Stancliffe

The Psalms, or certain of the psalms, have had a regular place in the daily prayer of Christians from earliest times. They constitute the nearest to a Jewish "hymnbook" that exists, and phrases of the psalms were on the lips of Jesus. Together with Second Isaiah, the Psalms provide the quarry for many of the texts which the New Testament writers used to explain Jesus' fulfilment of messianic prophecy. Understanding the Psalms as a whole in this way is deep-seated in the Christian tradition, and we can be confident that praying the Psalter is an unbroken tradition of Christian prayer which stems from Jesus himself and which links us directly with our Jewish forebears in the faith.

But how should we use the Psalter in our worship? Should we use only the psalms we like and ignore those we find difficult or uncongenial? Should we say them in course or select those appropriate to particular days or seasons? And what about those other well-known passages in the Old Testament which have the character of canticles, like the Song of Hannah, or of Miriam; or the Song of Jonah or of the Servant in Isaiah? And what relation should these passages have to the New Testament Canticles, the Song of Mary, the *Magnificat*, or the Song of Christ the Servant in Chapter 2 of the Epistle to the Philippians, or those in the Revelation of John?

Celebrating Common Prayer uses these ingredients to shape the Church's daily offering of prayer and praise in a distinctive way, including a wide variety of scriptural canticles from the Old and New Testaments, the regular use of the Lukan Gospel Canticles in Morning, Evening and Night Prayer, and a novel arrangement of the Psalter.

The Book of Common Prayer has preserved in the Anglican tradition the monastic pattern of reciting the whole Psalter. In the BCP the Psalms are recited in order during the course of a month, while in the developed Benedictine tradition, with seven Offices per day, the cycle is traditionally repeated each week. But while there is something to be said for the appropriateness of such a random method in rehearsing the different moods and experiences of human beings before God, reciting the whole Psalter in course was not the primitive practice, nor does it take any account of the suitability of certain psalms to certain days or seasons, let alone their traditional points of reference. Using such an arrangement you might find yourself reciting Psalm 51 on Christmas morning, for example; and would not Good Friday seem odd without Psalm 22?

So, alongside the tradition of reciting the Psalms in course has developed a pattern of "special psalms" – of chosing certain psalms for certain days and seasons, to help reinforce the mood and rhythm of the liturgical year. This is a pattern which has re-emerged in recent years for a number of reasons. Firstly, there is the experience of using short passages of appropriate psalms in the Ministry of the Word in the Eucharist. Secondly, much liturgical scholarship in the last twenty years has been devoted to exploring the earlier patterns of daily common prayer in the centuries when this was still very much the prayer of the whole people of God, and before it became the specialist preserve of the "professional" Christians, whether monastic or clerical. From this it is clear that the "cathedral" Office – the popular as opposed to the monastic form described for example in the writings of Egeria, a Spanish or French nun on an early pilgrimage to the Holy Land (*Egeria's Travels*, London: SPCK, 1971) – used only a limited number of psalms, and used them appropriately to the time of day, if not to the season. Psalms 95, 63 and 51, together with the *Laudate* Psalms – the psalms that begin with the phrase "Praise the Lord", Psalms 117, 146, 147 parts i and ii, 148, 149 and 150 – which were in regular use in Jewish daily prayer, figured regularly in the Morning Office, and psalms such as 141 and 104 were used each evening. A vestige of this survives in the use of Psalm 95, the *Venite*, as an invariable Invitatory psalm at Morning Prayer, and in the traditionally unchanging psalms for Compline – 4, 91 and 134. Such repetition is intentional: if the same psalms are repeated daily, they will soon be known by heart – a necessity in the case of Compline, which was said in the monastic dormitory in the dark; and if any prayer becomes known by heart, then it can be prayed, rather than read or listened to as information.

But it is not principally for "archaeological" reasons that *Celebrating Common Prayer* proposes a move in the direction of a more selective pattern for saying the Psalms. If we are serious about praying the Office, and encouraging others to pray it with us, then we must consider the appropriateness of the chosen psalms as well as the quantity in each Office. And this is where the proposals in *Celebrating Common Prayer* are distinctive. For a start, there are certain psalms which are repeated regularly each day of the week or each season as the Opening Canticle: each Thursday morning, for example, and each day in Epiphanytide, begins with Psalm 67. Sometimes this "canticle" – and we hope that much of the Office will be sung – will not be a complete psalm, but a selection of verses which makes a good whole. Then there is a regular repetition of certain psalms in certain seasons: for example, Psalms 33, 105, 114, 118 and 136 are used regularly in the weeks of Eastertide and on ordinary Sundays, but in the weeks of Advent Psalms 50, 70, 76, 80, 94 and 130 predominate. A series of psalms, repeated each week, gives a different flavour to the season, and enables the worshipper to become familiar enough with them to pray them.

These are only examples, but they serve to illustrate a different way of using the Psalter. For a start, not every psalm is used; and secondly, several psalms are used more than once in the Psalter table. This may sound strange to those who are used to reading the Psalter through in course, but no one would dream of singing all the hymns in the hymnbook, let alone doing it in order. We have chosen appropriately to the day and season.

There are some psalms which do not appear either in the table or among the special psalms. Psalms 14 and 108 are substantially doublets of 53 and 57 respectively, and so are excluded. So are the "cursing psalms": omitted entirely are Psalms 58, 60, 64, 83, 109 and 120, which are almost impossible to use in an Office where the emphasis has shifted in the direction of the praises of God and away from the informed reading of the whole of Scripture in course. But there are those who would argue for the retention of the whole of the Psalter in the Office on the grounds that it provides an unparalleled expression of the whole gamut of human feelings when confronted with the reality of God. So we have made it possible for virtually the whole Psalter to be read in an alternative table on pages 688–689.

Another category which is difficult to use is the long narrative or historical psalm. No one who knows Handel's oratorio *Israel in Egypt* would want to be without Psalm 105, but forty-five verses is quite a chunk of psalmody at one go. And what about Psalm 78? Seventy-two verses would seriously overbalance the Office, and that kind of narrative psalm where dark sections alternate with lighter passages cannot easily be split into satisfying parts without losing the sense of drama. Perhaps the answer is to read psalms such as these dramatically in Vigil rites, when a congregation can settle to a more reflective style of participation.

There is another category of psalms which finds little place in the regular order – what we might describe as the psalms of personal superiority, where the righteous pat themselves on the back, sounding for all the world like the Pharisee in the Temple! So Psalm 37, for example, is not found in the regular table at all; nor – though for a different reason – is Psalm 49, a bleak psalm whose fundamental hopelessness seems alien to the spirit of true worship.

But what is much more significant for the whole pattern and feel of the Office is not the choice of psalms so much as their arrangement. As Morning, Midday, Evening and Night Prayer are printed out in full seven times from Sunday right through to Saturday, each Office has printed out a seven-week cycle of psalms. But because each day bears a seasonal thrust, when we come to a particular season like

Advent or Eastertide, then the Office for Tuesday is read every day in Advent, or Sunday's in Eastertide, and the seven-week cycle of psalms is read on the seven days of each week in the season. In the "green" seasons of ordinary time, therefore, each weekday takes on a particular character which is further emphasised by the refrains, canticles, responsory and collects. During a special season a choice can be made between two or three seasonal canticles to give some variation.

The table below sets out the days of the week and the seasons in which each day's Office is used repeatedly:

Sunday	Eastertide	Celebrating Christ's victory over death
Monday	After Ascension to Pentecost	Life in the Spirit and the new creation
Tuesday	Advent	Preparing for the coming Kingdom
Wednesday	Christmastide	Celebrating the presence of God-with-us
Thursday	Epiphany to Candlemas	Revealing Christ to the world in mission
Friday	Ash Wednesday to Easter Eve	Returning to God and accepting Christ's cross
Saturday	All Saints to the Vigil of Advent	The end of all things, the vision of heaven, the promise of his glory

In this way, the weekly pattern in ordinary or "green" time offers a compact rehearsal of the two major liturgical cycles in the Christian year, and at the same time includes appropriate variables for each season. More than that, a complete pattern for daily prayer is being offered to clergy, religious and lay people alike, with everything set out ready for use.

The only additional preparation needed is to find the place in the Psalter and, for the reader, the place in the Bible.

The psalms are allocated over this seven-week, seasonal cycle with a degree of appropriateness to the seasonal flavour of the day. A "praise" psalm is assigned to each day at Morning Prayer, and the Opening Canticle – the Invitatory, as it has been called – uses well-known passages of psalmody appropriate to each day. At Midday Prayer, the traditional use of Psalm 119 is provided, with the Songs of Ascent (Psalms 120–134) as an alternative, with their historic association of a journey onward.

Within this overall framework, a particular character has been given to certain days and seasons – notably around Christmas, Holy Week and Easter and Pentecost – by the use of significant groups of psalms. We draw considerably on the *Hallel* (Psalms 113–118). The Jews customarily recite this at the great feasts; in addition, Psalm 136, the Great *Hallel*, is recited after the *Hallel* at the Passover; a third, or "lesser" *Hallel* (Psalms 146–150) is recited at their morning prayers.

We have also drawn on the Songs of Ascent which were almost certainly sung by pilgrims on their way to Jerusalem. Psalm 84 was probably used in the same way. In addition we have used where appropriate the Penitential Psalms, and the Kingship and Messianic Psalms (especially at Christmas and Epiphany, on other christological feasts, and on Palm Sunday). Other Jewish associations have influenced us; for example, the association of Psalm 92 with the morning of the Sabbath, of Psalm 30 with the Feast of the Dedication, and of Psalms 29 and 81 with the Feast of Tabernacles.

Many feasts have their proper psalms. In some way or another these psalms reflect either the themes of the feasts themselves, or the readings associated with those feasts. In many instances these psalms have a very long association with the feasts. In each case a "praise"' psalm is also provided each morning, chosen because there is some inner harmony between that particular feast, its readings, and that psalm. However, no "praise" psalm is allocated to Ash

Wednesday, Holy Week and All Souls' Day, all of which have a particularly austere character. On Ash Wednesday all of the Penitential Psalms are used since Psalm 51 is said as the Opening Canticle.

During Holy Week the psalms are largely drawn from those which have over the centuries been most intimately associated with the circumstances and details of the Lord's Passion. At Morning Prayer on Palm Sunday Messianic psalms, which are prayers for the king, are used.

During Easter Week, the whole period from Easter Day to Low Sunday, the *Hallel* Psalms are recited. They are spread as a whole over the two Sundays, and are coupled on weekdays with others which have a long association with the Lord's Resurrection.

During the eight days immediately before Christmas, *O Sapientia* to Christmas Eve, the morning psalms are from the *Hallel*, reflecting the near concurrence of Hanukah, and the evening psalms draw on the Songs of Ascents to express the sense of pilgrimage to the festival of Christmas.

During the ten days of Pentecost, from after Ascension Day to the feast of Pentecost itself, the Psalter draws on and combines four groups of psalms which look both backwards and forwards: first, the Kingship and Messianic Psalms which celebrate the universal sovereignty of God and the promise of his Coming which is partially fulfilled on the Day of Pentecost; secondly, the Zion Psalms which in eschatological tones hymn the glories of the Holy City, the dwelling-place of the Most High and the goal of pilgrimage; thirdly, the Songs of Ascent which express the notion of pilgrimage again; and fourthly, a number of psalms which in various ways help us to look forward to the theophany of Pentecost, the manifestation of the power of God in wind and fire.

The distinctive colouring given by this arrangement of the Psalter is reinforced by the choice of canticles from among a very extensive provision. At Morning and Evening Prayer a choice of two canticles is printed in each of the seven forms, one for more general use and one which is particularly suitable to the season. But there is an entire section of canticles, with thirty-five from the Old Testament and Apocrypha and thirty-one from the New Testament or later Christian writings. Included among these canticles are a variety of verse or song-like passages which are well known, like those from Isaiah 9 ("The people who walked in darkness . . .") and Isaiah 11 ("There shall come forth a shoot . . .") and which, through repeated use in a particular season, will soon become known by heart.

In the New Testament canticles too, there has been a selection of some of the more memorable passages which have a hymn-like quality, some of which – like the canticles in Philippians 2 and 1 Timothy 3 – may have had a pre-Pauline form. These combine with the Lukan Gospel Canticles and those from the Revelation to John to provide a varied New Testament selection, to which are added some hymns from the Christian tradition – the *Phos Hilaron* in a variety of translations, the *Te Deum* and *Gloria*, and songs from Anselm, Francis of Assisi and Mother Julian of Norwich.

The Gospel Canticles provide a climax to the psalmody, readings and canticles in the Office. The *Benedictus*, the *Magnificat* and the *Nunc Dimittis* provide a regular pattern which rehearses each day the mystery of the Incarnation. We move from the expectation of the coming of God among us at the start of the day in the *Benedictus* – the "Advent" canticle – to the celebration of what God has been doing (with or without our active co-operation) to raise up the lowly in the *Magnificat* at Evening Prayer, finally surrendering ourselves into sleep in the confidence of old Simeon's *Nunc Dimittis*, that Christ is the light of the world and that the whole creation is safe in his hands. This pattern of canticles from Luke's birth and infancy narratives earths the daily pattern of the Office in the prayer of the incarnate Christ to the Father.

In some contexts and on some occasions, these canticles will be replaced by hymns or other metrical songs. But the Office will form its own distinctive pattern of prayer best when a relatively small number of psalms and canticles become so well known that the worshippers become caught into their pattern of praise. To find oneself praying the Office without having to assimilate the material each time by an effort of conscious will is to draw close to that sense of losing oneself in the unending prayer of Christ to the Father which is at the heart of the experience of common prayer.

5 ◆ Celebrating the Church's year

MICHAEL PERHAM

The calendar in *Celebrating Common Prayer* (at least in its provision for Sundays and seasons) suggests modification to the Church of England's calendar of *The Alternative Service Book 1980* that draws on various other traditions. This may be seen as a first attempt at a draft of the calendar for the Church after the turn of the century. Before and after Christmas the *Celebrating Common Prayer* calendar relies heavily on the proposals in *The Promise of His Glory* (London: Mowbray/Church House Publishing, 1991), and for the period from Easter to Pentecost on the calendar of the Roman Catholic Church, but throughout the year there can be found a reverence for the calendar of *The Book of Common Prayer* that was not in the mind of the 1980 revisers.

In *The Promise of His Glory*, the Church of England's Liturgical Commission argued strongly for a rethink of the period leading up to Christmas. A four-week Advent was always in danger of being squeezed out by an encroaching Christmas. The ASB 1980 tried to remedy this with its "nine Sundays before Christmas", conscious that in Christian history Advent has been of variable length. *The Promise of His Glory* and the commentary on it (*Welcoming the Light of Christ*, London: SPCK, 1991) both argue that "the nine Sundays before Christmas" approach has not quite met the need, because it has ignored the traditional themes and flavours of that part of the year. The ASB provision, with its potted history of the Old Testament in five weeks, beginning with Creation and the Fall, and moving via Abraham and Moses, to the "Faithful Remnant", cuts across such observance as All Saints' Day and All Souls' Day, Remembrance Sunday and, for those in the Catholic tradition, the Feast of Christ the King. What is needed, *The Promise of His Glory* argues, is a calendar that takes these seriously and integrates them theologically and liturgically with the traditional Advent themes to which they do indeed naturally relate. *The Promise of His Glory*'s answer is to make All Saints' Day a "hinge point" in the Christian year, bringing to an end the "after Pentecost" period of ordinary neutral time, and inaugurating a pre-Advent season of the Sundays of the Kingdom, Advent in flavour, yet distinct from it, in which All Souls', Remembrance Day and the celebration of the kingship of Christ all have a natural place. *The Promise of His Glory* argues this strongly, and makes full liturgical provision for it, though its lectionary (following the Common Lectionary) does not always bear this out fully. *Celebrating Common Prayer* takes this argument on board without reserve, and provides for a season of the Kingdom from All Saints' Day. Its only departure from *The Promise of His Glory* is in the numbering of the Kingdom Sundays, where it regards the Sunday after All Saints' Day, even when it is kept as All Saints' Sunday, as the first of the Kingdom Sundays. On this reckoning, there are four Sundays of the Kingdom, not three as in *The Promise of His Glory*.

Celebrating Common Prayer also follows *The Promise of His Glory* in its provision for the period from Epiphany to Lent. This centres around the significance given to Candlemas, the Feast of the Presentation (2 February), where a change of direction occurs. Until Candlemas, the provision looks back to Christmas and the Feast of the Epiphany, and, in an extended Epiphany season, celebrates and reflects upon aspects of the Incarnation and the revelation of Christ through such events as his baptism in the Jordan, and the turning of water into wine at Cana. Thus the Sundays are designated "*of* Epiphany", not "*after* Epiphany". That Epiphany season continues until Candlemas, however early or late Easter is to be, but on 3 February there begins a pre-Lent season, of variable length depending on the date of Easter, with something of the same feel as the old "Gesima" Sundays of the BCP. Because *Celebrating Common Prayer* does not provide a eucharistic lectionary, it will be left to later revisers to develop the ethos of this pre-Lent season. There will be a case for the restoration of the creation emphasis, traditionally attached to Septuagesima, moved in the ASB to the Ninth Sunday before Christmas, but lost in *The Promise of His Glory*'s proposals. Some would also claim that the Transfiguration would be better placed (as in the American *Book of Common Prayer* 1979) on the next Sunday before Lent rather than on Mothering Sunday.

In its provision before Easter, *Celebrating Common Prayer* attempts to clarify an element of confusion about "Passiontide". Neither the BCP nor the ASB designates the Fifth Sunday in Lent as "Passion Sunday", though this has been its popular name. The Roman calendar calls the Sunday before Easter "Passion Sunday", while Anglicans call it "Palm Sunday". The ASB seems uncertain whether Passiontide material begins on Lent 5 or on Palm Sunday. In the Roman provision, it is clearer. Passiontide is synonymous with Holy Week, and there is no significant shift at Lent 5. *Celebrating Common Prayer* holds the line in not calling Lent 5 "Passion Sunday", which would be ecumenically confusing, but nevertheless places that Sunday clearly in "Passiontide" and envisages a significant change of gear at that point. As the notes to the Season of Passiontide express it: "Although Passiontide forms a part of Lent, the propers change to give a greater emphasis on Christ's suffering."

The most striking departure from previous English Anglican provision is in the treatment of Eastertide in *Celebrating Common Prayer*. The change comes first of all in the names of the Sundays. They are Sundays "*of* Easter", not "*after* Easter". This is not simply a tidying-up exercise. All too often communities do not even attempt to sustain the paschal flavour of worship through the weeks *of* Easter until Pentecost, but soon relapse into a kind of neutral unfestal ordinary time until Ascension Day appears. The Fifty Great Days, from Easter Day to Pentecost, are a gradual unfolding of the Easter mystery, and the whole season is held together by its distinctive paschal character. Sundays "of Easter" are numerically out of sequence with Sundays "after Easter" – The Sunday after Easter Day becomes "The *Second* Sunday of Easter", rather than "The *First* Sunday after Easter", and it may have been this bit of potential confusion that caused

48

the ASB 1980 revisers to hold back, but the change is crucial to a proper understanding of the season.

More fundamental, however, is the relationship to Easter of both Ascension and Pentecost. Previous Anglican calendars, including the ASB, reveal two models in competition, with ensuing confusion. One is of successive seasons of differing length – Easter (forty days), Ascension (ten days) and Whitsuntide (seven days,), the one leading into the next, but each fairly distinct in what is celebrated and in its liturgical texts. The BCP sees it like this. The ASB sometimes sees it like this, but at other points seem to be accepting another model. This is of a single fifty-day season, taking in Ascension Day and ending on the Day of Pentecost, with ordinary neutral time beginning on the day after Pentecost. In this single season the Easter mystery is unfolded, with an emphasis on the "going to the Father" element in the days leading up to Ascension Day, and an emphasis on the gift of the Spirit in the days from after Ascension Day till Pentecost. On this model Pentecost is not a seven-day season of a week, beginning on Whit Sunday, but a ten-day sub-season of Easter, culminating on Whit Sunday. *Celebrating Common Prayer* opts whole-heartedly for this latter model, which is the more primitive, and which is also the one to which the Roman Catholic Church has now returned. The very day after the Day of Pentecost, the neutral "green" time "after Pentecost" has begun, although it is soon interrupted by Trinity Sunday and by Corpus Christi.

In its approach to the Saints' days, the *sanctorale*, *Celebrating Common Prayer* is far more tentative. It divides its monthly calendar into two parts "above and below" an imaginary line. Above the imaginary line, in large type, is the main calendar provision, and this is straight from the ASB, modified only by the provisions in *The Promise of His Glory*. Below the line, in smaller type, are some other suggestions. But *Celebrating Common Prayer* gives them this rather tentative status simply because they anticipate an important debate the Church of England still needs to have. By what process, that debate needs to ask, are names to be admitted to the Church's calendar of saints, and what does their inclusion mean? There is a general feeling that this question was not faced with any rigour in the Liturgical Commission before the ASB was produced. Certainly the General Synod deliberations revealed a lack of clear principle or procedure. The "below the line" provision does raise some of the questions and is also a first attempt to redress some imbalance.

One area that needs exploring is that of saints of our own century. The ASB followed an earlier Anglican convention of not admitting any names to the calendar for fifty years after death. In fact Bishop Edward King, who died in 1910, and Josephine Butler, who died in 1907, were the sole named representatives of the present century. Even under the fifty year rule, some new names might merit inclusion, and *Celebrating Common Prayer* includes four that have leapt the fifty year hurdle since the ASB was authorised – Charles Gore (1932), Evelyn Underhill (1941), Maximilien Kolbe (1941) and Simone Weil (1943) and two that would leap the hurdle before the turn of the century – Dietrich Bonhoeffer (1945) and William Temple (1944).

But does the fifty year rule make sense in any case? In earlier centuries sanctity was recognised and celebrated in local communities as a spontaneous and often speedy response to the death of a Christian hero or heroine. A cult would very probably have taken fifty years to become widely known, but in these days of world-wide communications the local can so much more easily become the universal. Is there a case for the inclusion in the calendar of more recent Christian martyrs, like Janani Luwum (1977) and Oscar Romero (1980), and others who have shaped the Church or its theology in our own day — Pierre Teilhard de Chardin (1955), Michael Ramsey (1988), Pope John XXIII (1963), George Bell (1958) or Thomas Merton (1968)? *Celebrating Common Prayer* would encourage those who wish to explore their commemoration in the liturgy.

Another area of concern is the place of women in the calendar. Traditional calendars, including the ASB, have a strong masculine bias, and, if women find a place, it is more often for living as a chaste religious than for any other vocation, and sometimes patronisingly for being a "wife and mother". Neither Thomas More nor George Herbert are described as "husband and father", for all the importance they attached to family life. The *Celebrating Common Prayer* calendar celebrates a larger number of the great women of Christian history, some of them women of great power and influence conveniently forgotten through recent centuries. Nearly every month includes a significant new name that affirms the feminine, some of the names well-known, others obscure to those who have not been aware of some of the "rediscoveries" made by the contemporary Christian women's movement. The possibilities include Gladys Aylward (1970), Joan of Arc (1431), Angela de Merici (1540), Elizabeth of Portugal (1626), Mary Sumner (1921), Florence Nightingale (1910), Hildegard of Bingen (1179), Elizabeth Fry (1845), Elizabeth of Hungary (1231), Mechtild of Magdeburg (1280) and Jane Frances de Chantal (1641). There are more.

At the same time there is a conservative instinct at work to restore to the calendar the names of holy men and women whose stories or patronage are part of our Christian culture, some of it at "folk religion" level. Many of the names in the BCP and 1928 Proposed Prayer Book calendars are restored among these additional commemorations, not least because of the number of churches in England and elsewhere that carry their name. So the provisions include St Sebastian, St Valentine, St Richard, St Margaret and St Cecilia. The way that festivals are celebrated also give a higher profile to the patron saints of the British Isles, putting David, Patrick and George on a par with Andrew and other apostles.

Among other changes at which the calendar does little more than hint is the celebration of the festivals of the Blessed Virgin Mary. Many Anglicans regret that, at the eleventh hour, the General Synod placed the major feast of Mary on 8 September, traditionally the day of her birth, rather than on 15 August, traditionally her principal festival and the day of her entry to heavenly glory. The choice was of course to avoid any association with an unbiblical doctrine of Mary's "assumption", but it has left the Church of England in the odd position of providing liturgical material celebrating the end of her earthly life on a day when the majority of the Church is celebrating her birth. *Celebrating Common Prayer* suggests a move into line with other churches on both 15 August and 8 September.

Celebrating Common Prayer makes richer provision than the ASB for collects, but the ASB is its basic source. As far as the *temporale* (the seasons) is concerned, the ASB collect has been used except in two sets of instances.

The first is where the ASB is highly thematic. This is not only where the ASB theme has been lost in the new calendar (as, for instance with Abraham on the Seventh Sunday before Christmas or the Word of God in the Old Testament on Advent 2), but at any point where the collect goes beyond a general seasonal flavour to a specific theme. Thus, for instance, the ASB's specific collect about healing on a Second Sunday before Lent gives way to one that is more general but with a hint of a healing theme, and its specific collect about the Transfiguration on Lent 4 is replaced with one that widens the reference to the approaching Passion. Just occasionally the deviation from the ASB is to *strengthen* the seasonal emphasis where this is lacking, as for instance on the Fifth Sunday of Easter where the ASB's rather neutral collect is superseded by one of a more directly paschal character (used by the BCP three Sundays earlier).

The other set of changes is where the ASB's collect is theologically thin. In most cases this means a return to the BCP collect, usually in a slightly modified form. Christmas Day, the Epiphany and Candlemas have all been treated in this way. Comparing the ASB collect with the BCP collect (modified) for the Presentation:

ASB	CCP
Almighty Father, whose Son Jesus Christ was presented in the Temple	Almighty and everlasting God, clothed in majesty,
and acclaimed the glory of Israel and the light of the nations:	We pray that as your only-begotten Son was this day presented in the Temple,
grant that in him we may be presented to you	In substance of our mortal nature,
and in the world may reflect his glory;	So we may be presented to you with pure and clean hearts,
through Jesus Christ our Lord.	by your Son Jesus Christ our Lord . . .

It is not difficult to see which goes straight to the theological point, but hard to understand why the ASB so easily abandoned BCP texts which had a long history even before they found themselves in the 1662 book.

Otherwise the ASB's Sunday collect provision is followed, but with two sorts of textual amendments. One is to make all language inclusive according to the guidelines in *Making Women Visible* (London: CHP, 1988). These particular proposals to meet the charge of excessively masculine terminology, that left many women feeling excluded, looked in each case for a substitute word or phrase that retained the rhythm of the prayer as well as the essential meaning. Thus "mankind" becomes on Lent 5 "the world", on Palm Sunday "the human race" and on Pentecost 3 "your children". Such an approach avoids the crudity of automatically substituting "humankind" for "mankind" and "people" for "men" without sensitivity to context.

The other textual amendment is, while retaining the ASB scheme of when each collect is used, to return more closely to the rhythms of the BCP translation of which it is a modification. Thus for Ascension Day, the BCP has:

Grant, we beseech thee, Almighty God,
that like as we do believe thy only-begotten Son
our Lord Jesus Christ
to have ascended into the heavens . . .

The ASB has:

> Almighty God,
> as we believe your only-begotten Son
> our Lord Jesus Christ
> to have ascended into the heavens . . .

Celebrating Common Prayer restores the Prayer Book's rhythm and resonance:

> Grant, we pray, Almighty God,
> that as we believe your only-begotten Son
> our Lord Jesus Christ
> to have ascended into the heavens . . .

It is all part of a renewed concern, not only to rehabilitate BCP material that was in danger of being abandoned, but also to seek a richer and more poetic liturgical language.

Whether in the year 2000, the Church of England will want to use the ASB scheme of collects as its basis is doubtful. The compilers of *Celebrating Common Prayer* did so in order to make it easier for people to use the two books together, but these proposals may be only transitional.

Where gaps have been created by the removal of unsuitable ASB texts, they have been filled first of all by the use of modified BCP Sunday collects that the ASB had displaced, but also by resort to, among other sources, *The Promise of His Glory* and the Canadian *Book of Alternative Services*. But there is little new material in the *temporale*; it is nearly all rearrangement, restoration of BCP texts, and a concern for season rather than theme.

More radical is the work on the *sanctorale*. The greater holy days mainly follow the ASB, with just a few improvements, notably, for instance, on St Joseph's Day, where the ASB's banal "open our eyes and our ears to the messages of your holy will" has mercifully gone. But the collects for the lesser Festivals are nearly all new to Anglican provision. Some appeared in the earlier version of the Francisan Office

Book, though several of these have been revised, especially with the need for inclusive language in mind. Several use with great subtlety and effectiveness the writings of the saint concerned. A number that fall in seasons with a strong ethos of their own are careful to make sure that the holy day enhances the season rather than cuts across it. Thus the collect for the Conception of Mary has an Advent feel:

> Grant that, as we rejoice in his coming as our Saviour,
> so we may be ready to greet him
> when he comes as our Judge . . .

and that for St George a thoroughly paschal flavour:

> God of hosts,
> who so kindled the flame of love
> in the heart of your servant, George,
> that he bore witness to the risen Lord
> by his life and by his death:
> give us the same faith and power of love
> that we who rejoice in his triumphs
> may come to share with him
> the fullness of the resurrection . . .

These new collects also bring a new balance to the way God is addressed. If the collects that come out of the BCP tradition are nearly always addressed to an "almighty" "Lord" God, among these God is "gracious", "loving", "sustainer", "redeemer" and "deliverer", God of "compassion", "mercy", "peace" and "salvation". But there is only the slightest hint at feminine imagery, even on the Festivals of female saints. In general the collects are more cautious than some other parts of the book.

What they do proclaim with clarity is that collects need always to be inclusive prayers in the sense that they have a broad enough sweep to draw together the prayers of all the people. They will need to reflect the mood and the season, but they will also need to guard against being too specific. Those in *Celebrating Common Prayer* complement and enhance its calendar, and will provide a good starting-point for those who look for better collect provision in any official Church of England books at the turn of the century.

6 ◆ What shall we read from the Bible?

DAVID SILK

At the heart of our Christian faith and practice lies paradox – infuriating, intriguing and perplexing paradox. I believe in three Persons and one God; I believe in Jesus Christ who is of two natures and is yet one person.

Paradox extends into all our living and into all our dying, into the area of predestination and free will. Paradox extends into the issues which surround our understanding of the evident signs of revelation, inspiration and holiness to be perceived in the living traditions of other faiths, while we remain faithful to Christ, and witness to him as the universal Lord and Saviour. Paradox extends to the celebration of the sacraments, which at one and the same time are both a recognition and a sign of a commission, of an authority and graces already given and received, and yet also a means of receiving those gifts. And paradox extends to our understanding and use of Scripture, which is itself at the heart of Christian faith and practice.

It is a plain fact of history that the Church existed before the Bible was formed. It was the Christian community which gave birth to the books of the New Testament, and by its judgment invested them with an authority beyond that of other contemporary works dealing with the same subjects and claiming to be written by an apostolic hand. It was the Church which wrote, adopted and authorised the New Testament. And yet, at the same time, the books which were finally chosen to form the canon of Scripture clearly had some kind of distinctive, intrinsic quality and authority clearly recognisable apart from the Church. Furthermore, the Church has chosen, although she was once the judge of what should be counted as Scripture, to be herself under the discipline and judgment of those same Scriptures.

The placing of the Church under the direction and the

judgment of the Scriptures is clearly to be seen in the practice of adopting lectionaries. The use of a lectionary, with its course of readings dependent on the wisdom and choice of the wider Church, has a number of gifts to offer. First, the local church or congregation is bound into a wider fellowship, a binding which has a sacramental significance and character. Secondly, worshipping congregations are preserved from being subject to the whims and fancies of those who take the services. Thirdly, God is allowed to speak to us from the sacred texts with as little interference from us as is possible.

In short, to take and read and reflect upon what is appointed for a particular day, and to draw from it what God is saying to our particular situation on a particular occasion, means that we share the message with many other Christians, that we are exposed to the rich sweep of the whole of Scripture, and that there is less likelihood of our choosing to hear only what we want to hear.

The authority of Scripture over the Church is enhanced by the use of *lectio continua*, the practice of reading continuously through each book, as was the custom of reading the Law in the synagogue. This seems to have been a major characteristic of the usage of the early church, although evidence is incomplete and confused. The truth is that the selection of readings at the Eucharist was originally dependent on the bishop. On occasions this choice provided schemes of continuous reading, but not necessarily. In the fifth century St Augustine's sermons offer evidence for the selection of readings by the bishop while the readings for great festivals had already become fixed. There were no authoritative lectionaries until the mid-fifth century, and none for the whole year until the seventh. The lectionary principle, however, probably goes back into the New Testament itself. At least one scholar has found considerable evidence to show that the Synoptic Gospels are to be found in their present form precisely because they were put together as lectionaries.

A further necessity for Scripture to be pre-eminent in the

life of the Church is that a lectionary is compiled to cover a period sufficiently long to allow most of the Bible to be read. Thus, in the case of the Eucharist, it is quite impossible to do justice to the whole of the Bible in the course of a single year. *The Alternative Service Book 1980*, following broadly the proposals of the Joint Liturgical Group, departed from the general tradition of Anglican lectionaries established in the Book of Common Prayer by introducing a two-year course of readings and a thematic approach to selection. The new Roman Lectionary on the other hand, which has been adopted by the majority of the churches of the Anglican Communion, the greater proportion of the Lutheran Churches, and now on our own doorstep by the Church of Scotland, uses a three-year span and *lectio continua* to provide for an even richer selection of Sunday readings from Scripture.

The ASB provision is based on principles associated with the Biblical Theology Movement which was concerned to harmonise the books of the Bible, while the Roman (three-year) Lectionary is more obviously dependent on the work of Redaction Criticism, which is more concerned to do justice to the distinctive view of each author. It is then, for reasons of scholarship, as well as of fullness of doctrine and richness of spiritual experience, that the Liturgical Commission of the Church of England has placed the Three-year Lectionary at the scriptural heart of its provisions in *Lent, Holy Week, Easter* (1986), and in *The Promise of His Glory* (1991).

The Revised Common Lectionary (1992) harmonises the two approaches, and reconciles them in one provision, but it is based fundamentally on the three-year scheme. It is a eucharistic lectionary only, and, while it generally offers *lectio continua* for the Epistles and Gospels, it offers a dual course from the Old Testament, the one thematic and the other continuous.

The present proposals for the Daily Office develop that approach in the light of experience of the use of *Lent, Holy Week, Easter* and *The Promise of His Glory*. Even when we provide readings to reflect one of the themes of a particular observance, we prefer to allow the character of each biblical author to emerge by providing a whistle-stop tour of a book, or section of a book, rather than selected readings from a number of books. This is a lectionary scheme which is similar in its principles to, and compatible with, the Three-year and Revised Common Lectionaries on the one hand, and with the BCP lectionary on the other. However, those who use the lectionary of the ASB will need to make only a few minor adaptations, particularly in the case of festivals.

Although this is a lectionary which is closely allied to the calendar we have adopted, and is most naturally to be used with the Roman or Common Lectionary (so-called because it is the result of international ecumenical co-operation) at the Eucharist, this Daily Office can quite easily be used with the two lectionary provisions authorised for use in the Church of England, that of the BCP with the 1961 lectionary or that of the ASB. It is also generally compatible with the lectionaries authorised in the Church in Wales, the Church of Ireland and the Scottish Episcopal Church. We have naturally taken particular account of the use in those sister churches in our provision for the patron saints of their nations.

Celebrating Common Prayer does not follow in detail the calendar of the Roman Catholic Church: it follows in the Daily Office the calendar of *The Promise of His Glory* for the period from All Saints' Day until Candlemas, and adopts the mainline Anglican and Western tradition for the rest of the year (except Pentecost).

Although the year begins with Advent Sunday, it is convenient to begin our thinking earlier in November, and to provide for the weeks of the Kingdom, the period at the end of the old cycle which turns its back on Pentecost and looks forward to Advent and reflects the mood of the dying year. This begins with the season around All Saints' Day. The weekday and Sunday readings for the Kingdom Season and Advent are continuous until Advent 3, and then the particular readings appropriate to the approach to Christmas begin.

After Christmas there are a number of readings to fill the period to the Epiphany and the Baptism of Christ, and from then continuous reading resumes until Candlemas.

After Candlemas the Church turns towards Holy Week and Easter, and the readings are assigned by working backwards from Shrove Tuesday. This is the first of our concertinas – periods which will be longer or shorter depending on the variable date of Easter. In the Roman Lectionary there is only one concertina. From Epiphany 1 the lectionary runs forward from The Baptism of Christ (Epiphany 1) and stops at Shrove Tuesday; it is then counted backwards from Advent Sunday until the readings begin after Pentecost; the weak point of the concertina provides for the omissions for the year to be between Shrove Tuesday and Pentecost. In the provision of the Common Lectionary there is a rather more complex procedure to meet the need for flexibility, although it follows a basically "Roman" approach. In our provision, because Candlemas is a crucial festival in every sense of the word, we run forward from Epiphany 1 and backwards from Shrove Tuesday to give a more coherent pre-Lent pattern. The omissions are at Candlemas. Another concertina occurs later in the year.

Lent follows, and Holy Week and Easter are observed, as is traditional and customary, with Eastertide culminating in Pentecost. The days between Ascension Day and Pentecost are designated "Pentecost". They are observed as days of prayer and preparation for the Coming of the Holy Spirit at Pentecost, and the week after Pentecost (the old Octave) is no longer observed, thus following a more ancient tradition. Regular reading begins again on weekdays after Pentecost Sunday, and on Sundays after Trinity Sunday. It continues for fifteen weeks; that is the average period required to feature some major books of the Bible on Sundays.

Then the second concertina appears. The readings are appointed by working backwards from All Saints' Day, and the weak point of this concertina always falls around the beginning of October. This date also connects quite well to the natural rhythm and pattern of life by relating to the general resumption of many things social and academic after the holiday season.

The Sunday course of readings effectively begins with the Kingdom-Advent 3 provision. The note of the season is essentially eschatological and apocalyptic. On the Sundays there is, after the celebration of All Saints, on the Second Sunday of the Kingdom, a set of single readings from the prophetic books and the Epistles. This is followed by courses of readings from the Old Testament and Apocrypha in Maccabees and Daniel (reflecting Jewish history in the period just before the New Testament era, and the coming celebration of the festival of Hanukah), First Isaiah, Zechariah, Amos and Second Isaiah; the New Testament affords three courses from the Revelation, and a selection from 1 Corinthians and the Gospels of Luke and John. Although the Fourth Sunday of the Kingdom may be observed as the Festival of the Kingship of Christ, the courses continue largely undisturbed except for the use of the accounts of the Lord's triumphal entry into Jerusalem, a feature of the lectionary at this time of year adopted by Cranmer in the Book of Common Prayer (cf. the Gospel for the First Sunday of Advent) and characteristic of the six-week Ambrosian observance of Advent in Milan, a use which has in some other respects influenced our choice of readings during this period.

The weekday course in this same period begins to look towards Advent. We read from Ezekiel with his vision of the return from Exile, from Amos and Micah looking for the Day of the Lord, and from Ecclesiastes which has in Anglican tradition a close association with the dying year and the week before Advent. The New Testament course draws on Ephesians with its particular emphasis on the pre-existent and cosmic Christ, and its reference to the day of redemption, and continues reading in the Gospel of Matthew. In Advent we use both First and Second Isaiah, continue in Matthew through to the eschatological chapters, and read two Epistles to the Thessalonians, which of all Paul's letters feature a strong sense of the immediacy of the Lord's coming.

From 17 December to the Baptism of Christ (the First Sunday of Epiphany) the readings are generally allocated on a thematic basis, although there are some short runs of consecutive readings, whistle-stop tours. Before Christmas the twin themes of the Two Comings of Christ are explored, drawing much from Second Isaiah and the Revelation.

After Christmas the readings are devoted to theological reflection on the festival, using some key passages from the Gospel of John until the Naming of Jesus. Around the Epiphany we read from the Servant Songs of Second Isaiah and their note of mission to the Gentile nations, a few Gospel selections which continue to develop the Incarnation theme, the Epistle to the Ephesians – for the mystery revealed is at the heart of the Epiphany themes and message – and in the Acts of Apostles and the first steps towards a mission to the Gentiles in the early church.

The Sunday readings from the Epiphany to Candlemas reflect a variety of ideas: Ruth, alluding both to the family ancestry of Jesus and to his Gentile origins; 1 Samuel, with the early life of Samuel; Ecclesiastes, Proverbs, the Wisdom of Solomon, God's Word and Wisdom incarnate in Jesus; Micah, whose vision is fulfilled in Jesus; 2 and 3 John, Titus and 2 Timothy which afford reflection on the Incarnation; and key passages from the Gospel of John developing the keynote Gospel for Christmas Day. After Candlemas we continue to read in the Books of Samuel for the rest of the ordinary year until Kingdom and Advent. Then we begin a similar course in the Books of Kings, and use Jonah, Esther, Hosea, 1 and 2 Thessalonians and 2 Peter, together with some Gospel mini-courses, all of which point towards the notes of suffering and penitence which will characterise Lent.

The weekdays from the Baptism of Christ to the beginning of Holy Week must be considered as a single whole. By a long and universal tradition the period before Easter, the Christian Passover, is characterised by the reading of the book of Genesis and the beginning of Exodus. Anglican practice also follows a tradition older and wiser than that of the Reformation in associating the season of Lent with the prophet Jeremiah, whose experience of sorrow and rejection was very close to that of Jesus and leads to the reading of Lamentations during Holy Week. Lent is too short to provide adequately for the reading of Genesis and Jeremiah, and it is not possible to resort to a parallel of the old "Septuagesima" usage (Ninth Sunday before Easter) by beginning to read them at Candlemas, since the variable date of Easter does not allow a convenient and consistent starting-point.

Genesis and Jeremiah therefore begin immediately after the Baptism of Christ, and the readings are arranged so that the omissions in the concertina do not seriously interrupt the flow of thought and narrative. For example, the closing chapters of the Jacob story must always be read, and the Joseph cycle begins after Ash Wednesday. Thus after the Baptism of Christ the daily readings begin four new courses: Genesis with the Creation narratives, incorporating the themes of light and water, leading to the Exodus; Jeremiah leading to Lent and Holy Week; 2 Corinthians with its opening reference to the lowly origins of the Lord; and Luke's beginning to Jesus' Messianic ministry. During Lent the Epistle to the Hebrews develops the Jewish sacrificial background to the Passion. The Sundays of Lent are provided with readings from Genesis, and with material appropriate to penitence and the Passion.

During Eastertide the readings are drawn from a number of appropriate sources: the Books of Moses – Exodus, Numbers and in particular Deuteronomy, which has a long association with the season – and Joshua; Ezra, Nehemiah and the restoration of the Temple; the Gospel of John; the Revelation with its vision of the glorified Christ; 1 Peter with its ancient Easter associations and 2 Peter; together with a selection of passages offering reflection on the Resurrection. The days from after Ascension Day to Pentecost are an opportunity for reflection on the Coming of the Spirit.

After Pentecost the courses from the books of Samuel and

Kings are resumed on Sundays, and the books as yet unused are to be found in courses on both Sundays and weekdays. There is provision for twenty-five Sundays thus completing the year until the Kingdom-Advent season. Since the calendar suggests that the Last Sunday after Pentecost (the last Sunday in October) might well be observed as the Dedication Festival, or indeed as another commemoration or observance, the lectionary provision is such that the readings for that Sunday may be omitted without violence to the course: they are either a postscript to the courses, or an appendix to their respective books.

Full provision is made for Holy Days and Saints' Days. The readings are primarily compatible with the Roman and Common (Three-year) Lectionaries, but a slight adaptation only will enable them to be used with the eucharistic provision of either the BCP or the ASB. Proper readings are included for some festivals which are not at present regarded as major occasions in either of those books. Usually this is because the observance has some particular feature which distinguishes it; it may be, for example, the celebration of a New Testament saint, or of a national saint of some importance.

On Holy Days and Saints' Days provision is made for evening Prayer on the Eve, or for a Vigil. This provision will not normally be used unless the day is observed as a major day; it may, for example, be the patronal festival of the diocese, parish or house, or be a commemoration of considerable local importance. Since at a Vigil the Gospel of the morrow may be proclaimed, at least one option available in our table is from a part of the New Testament other than the Gospels.

Saints' Days and Holy Days break the pattern of *lectio continua*. Since our lectionary tends to provide passages of Scripture which are reasonably brief, it will generally be possible for local usage to overcome the difficulty without interrupting the flow throughout the week. It may perhaps be appropriate to add the first reading to that of the previous day, and the second reading to that of the following day, so that space is made for the observance of a saint. An alternative device is to look ahead at the week's provision to ensure that, over the whole week, one of the less important readings is lost by judicious shunting.

This approach can also be used at the omission points in our concertinas. It is quite possible, and often desirable, to spread the loss of the six readings for one week over a period of, say, three weeks. Indeed, if our basic lectionary scheme were to be adopted officially by the Church of England, the Liturgical Commission might wish to explore the idea of the publication both of a basic lectionary *in toto*, and also of an authorised order for each year. This would make necessary adaptations according to the observance in each particular year, and make an edition for the year available in a reader-friendly almanac form.

The readings in *Celebrating Common Prayer* are generally shorter than those of previous Church of England lectionaries. There are two major reasons for this. Firstly, the scheme is simply designed to experiment with brief passages to allow more time and space for reflection and prayer, and therefore to broaden the appeal and accessibility of the Daily Office. What may be possible for those who live a life of some leisure, for example, is not possible for, say, a busy parish priest, or a lay person with a demanding job. Secondly, the lectionary provision of *The Promise of His Glory* allows for the readings to be transposed between the Eucharist and the Daily Office. It is thus necessary that passages are briefer, or are available in an abbreviated form. However, brevity has presented some very real problems. Where a long narrative must be read we have provided for that, but on occasions a patchwork of verses is offered as an alternative. When the office is said publicly this will require some careful preparation for the reading. Of course, there is nothing to prevent a reader from using the complete passage instead of the patchwork.

It is for these reasons of flexibility and accessibility that the Lectionary exists in four columns. There are normally four distinct courses of readings on each day, although on a few occasions it is appropriate to read the New Testament "across the page", rather than "down the page", as on 29–30 December. Even when the same book is the source of the readings in both Morning and Evening Prayer it is possible to omit the first reading at Evening Prayer without interrupting the flow, as on the days before Ascension Day. Thus those who wish to do so may read one, two, or even three readings at Morning Prayer, and only one at Evening Prayer. Or it is possible to read two Old Testament passages at Morning Prayer, with or without a New Testament passage; Evening Prayer may be rendered quite brief by using the New Testament reading and either omitting the second canticle, or reciting it after the psalms.

The Anglican tradition has always made a very substantial provision of Scripture to be read at the Daily Office. Since the basic Office is reduced to twice daily, morning and evening, the weight of reading associated with the Office of Readings in other traditions is borne in ours by Morning and Evening Prayer. The provision of a lectionary "in four columns" makes it possible for those who wish to do so to read the bulk of the daily provision at one or other of the two offices. It would be possible also to include non-scriptural readings at such a time.

The readings have on the whole been designed and tailored for liturgical use. This means that they sometimes end on a high point liturgically, even if that is not at the natural break in the text. For example, on the Dedication Festival we read from the Gospel of Luke 19.1–10. But, while one would normally complete verse 10, "the Son of Man came to seek and save that which was lost", the same passage on the Dedication Festival gains much in impact if we read, "today salvation has come to this house", and stop there. Who could doubt that the dramatic ending to the reading of the Passion in the Gospel of Mark must be, "Truly this man was the Son of God"? Reading for liturgical purposes requires a distinctive approach to the actual selection of verses and presentation.

Considerable use is made of the Apocrypha, just as in

other Anglican lectionaries. But, unlike some Church of England lectionaries and that of the ASB, provision for a canonical alternative, particularly on Sundays and Holy Days, has not usually been made. There are four reasons for this: first, it is not always easy to find an appropriate canonical alternative, and, in a three-year course, virtually impossible to avoid substantial repetition. Secondly, this lectionary is in itself an alternative, and the legally authorised options remain. Thirdly, the opportunity to transpose from morning to evening and vice versa makes it possible to avoid apocryphal readings if this is desired. Fourthly, the Apocrypha has considerable spiritual value, and should not be wholly bypassed. It is hoped that the whole provision will be tried as it stands so that its approach can be evaluated fairly in due course.

We present here, then, a lectionary in the traditional mould: *lectio continua*, but in a three-year form. Each writer in the Scriptures is allowed to speak for himself or herself, and the greater part of the rich treasure of the Scriptures is covered. This lectionary is offered for experiment. All liturgical texts need to spring from the genuine and authentic spiritual experience of a worshipping community, and experiment is therefore essential to the formation and maturing of rich and lasting provisions. This is never more true than in the case of the lectionaries. They have to be tried out so that adjustments can be made. Lectionaries have about them something of the ever-demanding nature of the Forth Bridge and require similar attention, repair, adaptation and embellishment, and this can only be done by usage. This provision will need at the very least a three-year trial, and then some considerable revision in the light of experience.

7 ◆ Prayer and work: a new approach to the midday office

BROTHER JAMES

The Story

One day a priest and a brother were driving from Portsmouth to Cambridge and got caught in a traffic jam. To pass the time, they began to discuss the "problem of the Midday Office". Midday Prayer is the shortest Office of all, and is scarcely known to most Christians. (It is the last remnant of the "little Hours" of the monastic round: Terce, Sext and None.) And yet, in the 1980 edition of the Office Book of our community, Midday Prayer is the most complicated Office of all. On a feast day in the season of Lent, for instance, it requires five fingers, two thumbs, and a quick intelligence to navigate ten minutes of prayer! The new Office Book on which we were working was to be simple, easy to use, a handy book for clergy and laity as well as friars and sisters. What then to do with the Midday Office . . .

It struck one of the travellers that Midday Prayer might be ransomed from the tyranny of seasons and festivals if it were to reflect more "worldly" concerns. At one level this would not be such a departure – in tradition, periods of intercession have often been tagged on to the short Offices during the day. It seems only natural that as the day runs its course, those who pray should be remembering men and women in their daily work, the suffering and the Church in its mission and action.

The travellers became enthusiastic. If Midday Prayer could be so conceived as to reflect the needs of the world around us, it might then present itself as the ideal short act of prayer for a banker or office worker. It could be an ideal act of prayer for the beginning or end of a meeting. It could slip into the handbag or jacket pocket of a traveller. It could become the basis for informal prayer in a house group. Some themes would commend themselves to social action

69

or justice and peace groups, others to family gatherings or inter-faith meetings. It seemed as though they really might be "on to something".

There was a moment of cold feet as the idea was shared and people asked, "What about Christmas? What about Good Friday? Surely we want a special form of Midday Prayer for days like these?" Two answers emerged: yes, and no. Yes – if one wanted a special Office for important days, then it would not be difficult to give the flavour by having a relevant reading and collect. No – on the great feasts of the Church's year, is it not more important than ever to remember the world into which Christ was born, the world for which Christ died, in its unlovely rawness? By resisting the "temptation" to accommodate seasons, those who use the Midday Office daily might find that it develops a rhythm of its own, a rhythm based in the wider world, a rhythm which complements and counterpoints the seasonal rhythm of the Church's year. Such is our hope.

At about this stage I came on the scene. I had oversight of the pre-noviciate programme at Hilfield friary, and during that winter (1990–91) we had several young men who could claim to be worldly-wise and "unchurchy". Being presented with the broad lines of the new Midday Prayer, they were keen to be useful. During a two-week period of brain-storming we listed between seventy and eighty concerns in the world around us which we thought deserved either prayer or heightened awareness or both. It was of course inevitable that we should hit on themes which are highly topical now, and which ten years hence may have passed into the museum of faddishness. That was an eventful winter: the Berlin Wall had fallen, the Gulf War was brewing, the Thatcher era was coming to a close. We would not have predicted the breakup of the Soviet empire. Who knows where AIDS, or unemployment, or the damage to the ozone layer will take us by 2000? There is a danger in pinpointing concerns too specifically: the world changes every day. If our prayer is based in the world, it too will be in continual motion. But there is an opposite danger in being too general and bland. We hope that we have been able to provide a framework which will draw our attention to transitory, and even contentious, issues, but that we have avoided being too specific, so that both our understanding may grow, and events may move on. We hope that our solution to this problem will be a service to those who pray, and that it will stand the test of time, at least in the short term. It does not bother me if people in 2050 look at our Midday Office readings and say, ''That's how they, in the early 1990s, saw the world.''

A Week of Days

If you look at the readings section of the new Midday Office, you will see that each day presents a general heading under which seven particular concerns are listed. The general heading is reflected in a "short reading" printed out in the text. The first "response" and the first of the collects which follow turn this heading into prayer.

The areas to which our attention is directed are as follows:

Sunday	Creation and New Creation
Monday	Communication and Cultures
Tuesday	Wealth and Work
Wednesday	Family and Community
Thursday	Health and Healing
Friday	Caring for the Needy
Saturday	Justice and Peace

It is immediately apparent that these highlight some of the major preoccupations of people at the end of the twentieth century. They may be things we are exploring and are unsure about. They are likely to be causes of concern to our neighbours, Christian or not. They are elements which, if we could only get them right, would point us forward towards a better world. They are legitimate areas of Christian concern about which our praying and thinking need to be informed, both by knowledge of what the Bible has to say, and by awareness of what is happening in the world around us. The meeting-place of the world with God's Word becomes the playground for God's Spirit. New intuitions, new pangs of conscience, new inspiration for living as followers of Jesus in a changing world – these are to be expected when we let the Spirit of God play havoc with our habitual ways of seeing things.

Sunday – Creation and New Creation

Concern to preserve the ecology of the planet was once left to the small "green" fringe of church and society. Now it is a serious issue for world governments. How much more should Christians take seriously the imperative to care for an environment which we believe God created for us!

God calls us to be stewards of his gift. We unite ourselves with the creation in its worldless praise of God: "All you works of the Lord, bless the Lord, praise and glorify him forever." Much of today is taken up with simple praise and wonder as we contemplate God's works. Some of it evokes our longing for the day when the broken world will be restored, when "they shall not hurt or destroy in all my holy mountain" (Isa 11.9). And a mention of the Sabbath reminds us that we too are God's creatures, that the law of our being requires rest as well as activity, and that while we rest God will continue to hold the universe in being.

Monday – Communication and Cultures

We are perhaps the first generation to be so aware of the interconnectedness of people around the world. Even our own society is multi-racial, multi-cultural, multi-faith. It is no longer possible or desirable to keep those who are different from us at a distance. How can we continue to affirm the uniqueness of Christian faith, and yet open our hearts to those who do not share it? How can we delight in the distinctiveness of minority cultures while yet encouraging them to be part of something bigger?

The covenant between God and Noah is a universal covenant: it declares God's care for all people as well as for the whole creation. It is a covenant which is rooted deeper than all distinctions. And Habakkuk's vision of an earth "filled with the knowledge of the glory of the Lord" (Hab 2.14) must include all.

The joy of men and women from every nation, speaking different tongues and yet understanding each other is celebrated in Acts 2. The Pentecost story is a reversal of Babel's curse (Ge 11). The biblical message points us beyond present fragmentation to one world, one community, in which all acknowledge and worship the one God.

Communication across the different thought-worlds and cultures is the work of the Holy Spirit, the "go-between God". We focus on the media: who is it that gives us news we can trust? The incomplete news which Ahimaaz brings to David is welcome because David does not want to hear the whole truth (2 Sa 18.28−30). The only truly good news is life-giving because it changes our relationship with God and with others (Isa 52.7). Travel is another way of crossing boundaries, physical and cultural. The people of God have always been on the move, "seeking an abiding city" (Heb 11). Jonah and Paul are singular examples of those whose calling is to face alien cultures with words of life.

By education, we learn to appreciate the insights handed down to us in our own culture and faith community. Christians need never fear the search for truth, for we trust the Holy Spirit who leads us into all truth. Artists, musicians, poets, sculptors can, by tapping fresh creative springs, inspire us to recognise both the divine and the demonic in human experience, and so invite us to a praise of God which transcends language.

The question of other faiths is a particularly sensitive one. Are dialogue and evangelism opposed? Does worship which mixes Christians and others deny implicitly the uniqueness of Christ? For my part, I feel compelled to recognise holiness when I meet it in men and women of the great faiths, and to own it as the work of the Holy Spirit. Idolatry is a danger in all religions, including our own. It is clearly inappropriate to apply Biblical warnings against idolatry to other faiths, as though "false gods" equals the deities of non-Christian religions. If this premise is accepted then there is surprisingly little in Scripture that addresses the issue of Christianity's relationship with other faiths. The texts chosen imply a way forward without in any way prejudging the issues.

Tuesday – Wealth and Work

Work is an essential ingredient of our lives, both as individuals, and as a society. Who works? Who is denied the opportunity to work? Who benefits from an individual's labour? What sorts of work are valued in our society? These are a few of many questions which demand our attention.

Our exploration of wealth and work begins with a positive conviction: God acted in creation, and God's action was good. The goal of our productive activity is to co-operate with God in creating a good world, a healthy environment in which to live and die. However, we are all too aware that we live in a fallen world, a world in which things go wrong, in which tremendous amounts of energy can be expended towards evil ends. The perception of work as a curse is a reflection of this (Ge 3.17–19). The issues which result are symptoms of our wrong relationship with God, with the environment, with one another.

Productivity is good (Ps 65); it is a natural expectation (Lk 13.6–9). But the production of wealth can lead to an inequality which easily becomes injustice. A glance at the global economy reminds us that our attempts at wealth creation can have both good and bad effects on others. If our riches increase, so does our responsibility to use them well (Dt 15.7–11). "From everyone who has been given much, much will be demanded" (Lk 12.48, NIV).

Industry can cause pollution and put us into a wrong relationship with the natural world. It would be anachronistic to read our worries about the ozone layer back into biblical times, but people then interpreted plagues as indications of God's displeasure, and the parallel between pollution and plagues is instructive. Our wanton destruction of creation, our short-sighted using-up of resources for our immediate gain, has consequences from which God will not protect us. The price for a healthy environment is conversion of life. God calls us to "return", to be converted, or we will meet him in judgment (Am 4.9). God's pledge to Noah that he will never again curse the ground on our account, although it expresses the confidence that God will uphold the world in its integrity in spite of human wickedness, nevertheless falls short of pledging to protect us from the consequences of our folly.

Work raises questions of power. Power can be an oppressive thing, feeding on the work of others, to no good purpose. The parable of the trees in Judges 9.8–15 expresses this vividly. Or power can empower others, serving them and enabling them to serve. Jesus chose the latter way (Mk 10.45). Is this a realistic option for those in authority in our time?

Our society is plagued by the seeming opposites of unemployment and overwork. Some are blamed for having nothing to contribute, others are under such stress that they forget how to play. In fact, unemployment causes its own stress, anxiety and guilt. The sort of unemployment which is a symptom of our society was unknown in the Bible, but those who found themselves on the edges and unable to enjoy the society's full benefits would serve as a rough equivalent. The proclamation of a year of jubilee, good news for the poor and oppressed, on the lips of Jesus (Lk 4.18–19) is surely meant for our own disadvantaged. And Jesus' call to let go of anxiety and trust God for each day's need must be good news for us all.

Wednesday – Family and Community
We are all born. We grow up. The environment in which this happens leaves its indelible mark on our personalities, for good or ill. Our ability to enter into and sustain satisfying relationships can make of life a blessing or a misery. Yet it is remarkable how many families in Scripture are flawed. Jesus' most frequent comment on family ties is to call people away from them!

Our exploration of family takes us through the stages of life, from infancy through parenthood to old age, asking us to see how each can be given to God. The Scriptural blessing on those who choose not to marry is recalled, alongside an exuberant celebration of both the physical and spiritual joys of marriage. Realism and compassion require that attention be directed to broken families. (The two examples in *Celebrating Common Prayer* are of Hagar being sent away by Abraham and Joseph asking Benjamin to stay in Egypt: the story of David's adultery would have provided more shocking material!) The stories of David and Jonathan, and of Naomi and Ruth, help us to affirm the significance of friendship in many people's lives, and to acknowledge that same-sex relationships can call forth love, loyalty and sacrifice in God's purposes. The experience of bereavement reminds us that every human bond has built into it the expectation of letting go.

Thursday – Health and Healing

A broken world lacks health, and the ailment is everywhere apparent. The healing of society's ills is a necessary Christian concern, reflected in the prayer that God will "make whole both people and nations" ("Collect for the Eighth Sunday Before Easter", *The Alternative Service Book 1980*). But on this day we focus on individuals who need to be brought to wholeness. For Jesus, the ministry of healing accompanies his ministry of preaching, a powerful pledge that God's new order makes a difference in the lives of ordinary men and women.

We begin by evoking gratitude for our physical existence: Christianity is an incarnational, "embodied" faith. The material world is good, and that includes our own bodies. God's purpose is that our bodies be a source of delight rather than shame. God's purpose is for our health.

But things go wrong, so that not only our physical being, but also our emotional and mental being, become a burden. People long for death, or wish they had never been born. Job understood this. Couples want to pass on the gift of life, but find themselves unable to produce children. Women from Sarah and Hannah to Elizabeth have pleaded with God. And how does this relate to that other tragedy: a child expected where no child is wanted?

Some illnesses are more socially disabling than others, such as loss of communication skills when the mind is still alert and active. HIV and AIDS carry a burden of social ostracism comparable with biblical leprosy. Some diseases are feared, protracted, painful; others annoy, then pass quickly. Health itself can become an idol and a paralysing preoccupation. The medical profession in our day faces difficult ethical questions. We give thanks for doctors, nurses, researchers; for those who practise natural forms of healing; for charismatic healers. Health in its full Christian sense is to be seen in the context of salvation: the whole person, freed from sin, to serve God in holiness.

Friday – Caring for the Needy

It is nothing new in Christian tradition to remember those in need. We remember those in prison, "as though in prison with them" (Heb 13.3) – whether their sentence is just or unjust is not ours to judge. We are blessed in caring for them, and find that Jesus identifies himself with them. We remember immigrants to this country, and others who live as minorities, valuing their contribution to our society. God's people have often found themselves living as strangers in a foreign land, sometimes valued, sometimes despised. We remember those who are victims, exploited by those more powerful, caught in a slavery figurative or real; those who are victims of violent crimes, of violent upbringing, of wars. The Bible is full of people with whom they can identify. We remember those who are victims of natural disasters, the vagaries of nature which make us ask, "Why does God allow this?" We remember those who for any reason are hungry and homeless and lacking in life's basic necessities: the statistics of those who suffer habitually in these ways are depersonalising. In prayer we identify ourselves with these lovable human people. God has chosen them to have a pre-eminent place in his Kingdom. We remember those who express care tangibly on our behalf: organisations like Oxfam, Christian Aid, the Red Cross and Red Crescent, UNICEF, the Church Urban Fund, the Society for Prison Reform. The list is long. We remember those individuals whose work brings them into constant contact with such great need: prison chaplains and other clergy, social workers, aid workers, therapists . . . again, the list is long. We remember all of these in particular on Fridays, associating them with the Cross, with the mystery of re-demptive suffering, with the love of God revealed in Christ crucified.

Saturday – Justice and Peace

The prophets longed for the days of the Messiah as a time when wrongs would be righted and injustices overcome. Jesus taught us to pray, "Your kingdom come . . . on earth as in heaven". As we contemplate the world around us, we too desire and pledge ourselves to work for a better world, a world in which God's will and God's love are more nearly reflected.

Today we allow ourselves to be righteously indignant about the persistence of particular injustices, and pray for those who seek to end them. Racial inequality and prejudice is one. Another is the prejudice which has for so long oppressed women in a male-dominated society. Another is the abuse of others, frequently children, for sexual gratifi-cation.

The manufacture and sale of arms still threatens world security and has complicated economic implications for both industrialised and developing countries. Refugees are created by wars, by racial and cultural tensions, by famine and economic decline, by politics: having lost their homes, to whom can they turn? People are imprisoned and tortured because in all conscience they are unable to live by unjust laws. And conflict is still necessary as we seek to combat wrongs. The peace which God promises is not a peace which avoids tensions, but a peace which embraces conflict in the power of Christ, and believes in a resolution which can include all.

Over to You

And so, a week of themes leads us to contemplate the variety of God's creative activity, and the mixture of joy and pain in our human response: sometimes sadly inadequate and selfish, sometimes inspiring and approaching the stature of our creaturehood "in God's image". I hope you will find that the regular praying of the Midday Office will nourish your sense of God at work in the world, and will support you in your commitment to do God's work in the world. The world needs converting. We need converting. But the God who calls is faithful, constant, reliable. God is the beginning and the end of all our prayer and striving. May the God of hope fill us with all joy and peace through the power of the Holy Spirit.

8 ◆ Doing the office: the place of rites and ceremonies

CHARLES MACDONNELL

Liturgy is not about texts written in books, but about the performance of words and actions "in church". The purpose of this essay is to examine the ways in which Christians have prayed in the past, not looking at the texts they have employed while celebrating common prayer, but rather at the ceremony which has served to give tangible expression to their context.

The Church of England has never laid down detailed ceremonial directions for the performance of its liturgy, apart from certain essentials. This has proved both liberating and problematic in the past. However, certain conventions of style have emerged as distinctively Anglican, instanced by the growth and development of suitable ways of *doing the Office*. Their re-emergence in a renewed Office can serve to restore common prayer once more to its place in the forefront of Anglican consciousness, together with the Eucharist, as the backbone of our spirituality.

All the Offices reveal one of the dominant themes – *Light*. One of the earliest pieces of ceremonial connected with the Evening Office appears to be the bringing in of the Vesper-light by the deacon. Drawn from the domestic devotions of early Christians and Jewish families, this household chore was swiftly given a symbolic interpretation. Our knowledge of the liturgy in Jerusalem in the latter part of the fourth century is well chronicled in the travel-diary of Egeria, who was a religious woman, probably a nun, from the Atlantic seaboard of France or Spain. She visited Jerusalem in the 380s and gives a fascinating account of the special features of the services there. It is clear from her narrative that the lighting of lamps was the essential *action* of the service of Evening Prayer. The early hymn *Phos hilaron* ("Hail

80

Gladdening Light'') which probably dates from at least the third century, may have been composed for this very setting. Alongside verses from Psalm 141, it forms the kernel of the evening service. The psalm is of interest here, not just because it makes overt reference to an evening sacrifice, but because it links the Church's worship to the evening offering of incense in the Jerusalem Temple, and with Christ's own dying on the cross at the close of Good Friday. Egeria's account is worth quoting:

> At four o'clock, they have *Lychonicon*, as they call it, or in our language, *Lucarnare*. All the people congregate once more in the Anastasis (Church of the Resurrection), and the lamps and candles are all lit, which makes it very light. The fire is brought not from outside, but from the cave — inside the screen — where a lamp is always burning night and day. For some time they have *Lucarnare* psalms and antiphons, then they send for the bishop, who enters and sits in the chief seat. The presbyters also come and sit in their places, and the hymns and antiphons go on. Then, when they have finished singing everything which is appointed, the bishop rises and goes in front of the screen (i.e., the cave). One of the deacons makes the normal commemoration of individuals, and each time he mentions a name a large group of boys responds, *''Kyrie eleison''* (in our language, ''Lord, have mercy'').
> (John Wilkinson, *Egeria's Travels*, London: SPCK, 1971. p123f)

In the West something of this ceremony survived in the New Fire, kindled at the paschal Vigil on Easter Eve. There is a clear connection between this ceremony and the famous Easter proclamation (the *Exultet*) and the blessings of light used in the new Evening Office.

In the Eastern tradition the office has retained these ''popular'' elements. In the Byzantine rite for Evening Prayer we find the same initial devotions: for after the appropriate section of the Psalter, what do we uncover, buried at the very heart of the Office, but verses from Psalms 141/2 and the hymn *Phos Hilaron*?

Perhaps the most conservative and the most influenced by monastic practice, in respect of the Daily Office, is the East Syrian Church. Evidently, here is an authentic survival of the People's Office, even if by the nineteenth century poverty and political circumstances had reduced its ritual splendour. The following account is from A J Maclean's book, *East Syrian Daily Offices* (London: Rivingtons, Percival & Co., 1849. pxviif):

> Two beautiful features of the East Syrian recitation of the psalms are the appropriate collects before each subdivision of the *Hulali* (psalm-grouping) gathering up the thoughts of the psalms, and the *Giyuri*, or farcing, (i.e., elaborating) of each psalm . . . In practice the psalms are said on weekdays in monotone and antiphonally, one person on each side, not necessarily a priest or deacon, taking each clause. They recite very rapidly . . .
>
> We must especially notice the anthems . . . these . . . are sung by all persons who can read Old Syriac, that is, generally speaking, by all who can read at all; for the people have a great idea of congregational worship, although the musical effect is not all that might be desired. Those who cannot read cannot, of course, join in the singing; but there are certain portions of the service, such as the Lord's Prayer, the *Lakhumara* (Hymn to Christ), Holy God, and Nicene Creed, which all can say . . ."

All this was accompanied by some movement, so that the Office was very much something performed and not just recited. There was, for example, after the introduction and doxology, the Kiss of Peace, which was repeated before the recitation of the Creed (which concluded the Office). The heart of the Office was celebrated with the clergy processing down to the *Bema*, a raised platform in the centre of the nave. The deacon recited the *Karazutha* (the Litany) below the *Bema*, first vesting in stole and girdle. (Here, perhaps, users of the new Office can take note, especially with the possible recovery of a diaconate within the Anglican Church.) There is clearly scope in the format of the new Morning and Evening Prayer for deacons to be given a full liturgical expression of their ministry, especially in the leading of the prayers and litanies.

Enthusiasm for the new forms is not intended to sweep away the use of the Offices in *The Book of Common Prayer*. Their felicitous structure and peerless language have rightly obtained pride of place in Anglican liturgy. One must admit, however, that even Choral Evensong has experienced a marked decline in recent years. Despite its basically "monastic" form, Anglican Evening Prayer retained a popular ethos not least from its measured pace and biblical didacticism. But one wonders whether a certain experimentation in the way in which it is performed might not be opportune. The simple insertion, at the beginning, of some verses from Psalm 141, and the singing of the *Phos Hilaron* at the bringing in of the Vesper-light, particularly on festivals, might restore some of the life in the ancient People's Office.

If most now confine their churchgoing to Sunday morning and the Eucharist, might there not be scope for developing Saturday evening as the Vigil of Sunday? The liturgical provision, including the proclamation of the Sunday Gospel, in the new Office might encourage preparation for the Sunday Eucharist in times when the old devotional disciplines (fasting, prayer, and confession) have experienced a steady decline in popular piety.

Such carefully devised and rehearsed Vigil liturgies might contribute to the re-establishment of non-eucharistic services as part of the mainstream of the Church's worship. Their evangelistic potential is not to be ignored if we wish to reach those on the fringe of church life. The beauty of the new Office is that its content can be conformed to many different styles of liturgical practice, something which is not always possible in home-grown special services.

In Morning Prayer, the dominant theme in the early tradition appears once again to be that of Light. In the Evening Office the light was Christ, which the darkness of this passing age (symbolised by the gathering gloom), could not overcome (Jn 1.5). The morning light, on the other hand, is a continual reminder of the resurrection, where the rising sun symbolises Christ's rising from the dead (Ps 19.1–6; Mal 4.2; Eph 5.14). The opening proclamatory prayers in the new Morning Office are to be seen in this context: a blessing of God for the return of the daylight, recalling to our minds that Christ is risen. This matches what we have seen with the prayer of blessing recited before the Vesper-light, which recalls the light of Christ in a dark world.

These two approaches to light, set within the natural rhythms of the day, form the essential elements of each Office, so the ceremonial which attaches to them could be designed to bring out these central themes. That is not to say that what follows (the psalmody, the canticles, readings and prayers) is of little importance or mere time-filling. The psalms and readings, after all, are the heart of the Church's continual *anamnesis*, the remembering of salvation-history. The prayers and litanies also, far from being an appendage, were in the early tradition the *raison d'être* of the Daily Office: bringing the needs of the Church and the world before God. The tendency in the monastic tradition of the West was to reduce the intercessions, attenuated to perhaps a triple *Kyrie*, and the collect. The earlier ("Cathedral") Office, on the contrary, was focused upon psalms and hymns of light, and the reciting of litanies.

The renewal of worship is not an exercise in liturgical "archaeology". Even if the early Church only had scriptural lessons in the Office at Vigils and feasts such a structure would not be deemed normal today. But there is every reason to think carefully as to how the lessons are read and psalms are recited, and where the intercessions are offered.

After a few years of experimentation with the new Office in my own rural parish in Cornwall, I should like to conclude by sharing a number of practical suggestions:

a) Singing can be better than saying. This might be a matter of taste and ability, but simple chanting can greatly enhance the basic text. "He who sings prays twice", said St John Chrysostom. There is no need for anything elaborate.

b) The setting is important. The new Offices adapt well for use "in choir", even with clergy attired in traditional choir habit. There might be good reasons in some parishes to retain the monastic style during the week-days, with the Office read antiphonally. Perhaps, the more dynamic "Simple Celebration" might be celebrated on Sundays and feasts. We have sung the Office in our Lady Chapel, which is devoid of chairs (apart from around the walls). So we stand throughout, apart from the readings. The focus for the attention is clearly the altar for the opening rites and the prayers, and a centrally placed lectern for the readings. A useful piece of furniture is an adapted cupboard (chest-high) on castors, with a book-rest (and small strip-light) on top. This is used not only for storing necessary books, but as a place from which the cantor(s) can sing.

c) The centrally placed lectern encourages the idea of gathering around to attend on God's Word, rather than being lectured to from the front. A finely bound lectern Bible can become an appropriate focus for attention. For the Sunday Vigil proclamation of the Gospel we have used a book of Gospels, which was placed at the beginning upon the altar.

d) Incense (where appropriate) may be offered at the traditional place, such as at the verses of Psalm 141 in the evening, and at the reading of the Vigil Gospel. The thurible can also be left burning in the sanctuary with no actual censing at all.

e) For the Vesper-light an acolyte's torch can be used, placed as the service begins near the head of the nave. If the congregation hold hand-tapers, they take their light from this. Standing in front of the Vesper-light and facing East towards the altar is an appropriate position from which to recite the litanies and other intercessions. There is much to be said for recovering the tradition of all facing Eastward for prayer. Although the Westward position has increasingly become the norm for the president at the Eucharist, careful consideration needs to be given to the direct opposite, when at Morning Prayer we are considering the dawning sunlight (in the East) as the symbol of Christ rising. And in the evening, the West, as in Baptism ("I *turn to Christ* . . .") is the realm of darkness, which we "renounce".

85

f) The various memorials and commemorations suggested for the conclusion of the Office provide ample opportunity for movement, procession, and participation by the congregation. For example, the Thanksgiving for Baptism for use on Sunday, has been inspired by the procession to the Baptistery in the Ambrosian (Milanese) Rite. This procession to a different place is very important; as an appendage to the Office this commemoration means shifting the liturgical focus away from the altar and lectern to the font.

It is not insignificant that the Daily Office was imposed as an obligation on the clergy of the Western Church at much the same time as the idea of clerical celibacy. Such a creeping "monasticisation" of the parish clergy came in part from lay pressure, suggesting that those who handled the holy mysteries must lead lives as conventionally "holy" as the monks. To a large extent the decline of the late Roman world and the increasing christening of barbarian nations restricted the actual performance of the liturgy to those who could read Latin. That process did not obtain in the Eastern Churches to the same extent. There, the clergy have never been under the obligation to recite the Daily Office and candidates for the priesthood are normally married men. Saturday Evening Prayer, as a preparation for Sunday, is very much a feature of Orthodox parishes, but is only ever celebrated with the congregation. The sight of the lone cleric, quietly muttering "his Office" in his stall, is not a feature of the Eastern. Nothing, in fact, would appear more bizarre to them, where worship remains congregational.

This congregational aspect of daily worship has, historically, been one of the best of Anglican traditions. The invitation from the compilers of *Celebrating Common Prayer* is that we use what we already possess within the vast store of liturgical poetry, of both East and West: the authentic voice of the Holy Spirit, who speaks through us "with sighs too deep" (Ro 8.26) when our own words fail. This is, after all what we mean by tradition, not of people, but of God;

that which is orthodox, meaning not just the right belief, but also the true glory; the right way of worshipping what we rightly believe in.

9 ◆ Root and resource for family and group prayer

CHRISTOPHER COCKSWORTH

Praying in the Home

"But as for me and my household, we will serve the Lord" (Jos 24.15, NIV). So said Joshua as he invited the people of Israel to renew the covenant at Shechem. The covenant was between the community and God but this wider community of Israel was made up of smaller communities led by those whose responsibility it was to care and to guide. The same pattern continues in the new covenant. "Sirs, what must I do to be saved?", asks the Philippean jailer (Ac 16.30–31, NIV). "Believe in the Lord Jesus", he is told. He does, and he brings his whole family to be baptised into the life of Christ and into the new community. At both Shechem and Philippi, membership of the new community is marked by a community action (renewal ceremony and Baptism) and commitment to the life of the community is shown by a sharing in its life of worship and prayer. The people of Israel are told to teach their children about the character of the covenant, and space is especially set aside for this in the Passover celebrations. They are told to talk about these things when they sit at home and when they walk along the road (Dt 6.7). The first converts to Christ on the day of Pentecost devote themselves to the community's prayers and common life. They gathered in each other's home to eat and praise together with "glad and sincere hearts" (Ac 2.47, NIV).

As other essays in this book will have shown, *Celebrating Common Prayer* is seeking to help the Christian community to pray *as members* of the community. The task over the next few pages is to reflect on how the book, especially in its Simple Celebration of the Office, may help household communities to pray, and to do so in ways which retain a relationship with the prayer of the Church. Inevitably, within the culture in which most of us find ourselves, this will generally mean some sort of family grouping. Of course, we must always remember that the biblical concept of a household is much larger than the nuclear family of modern times; we must be grateful to those who are experimenting with wider forms of Christian household and we must encourage nuclear families to be open and welcoming in their outlook. However, given the present character of family life and also the contemporary pressures even on the nuclear family to split into smaller groups, it seems worth concentrating on ways of helping parents in their various circumstances to pray with their children.

Families find it very difficult to pray together. Probably very little of it happens even amongst regular worshipping families. Dr Leslie Francis has shown that the practice of saying grace before meals is almost extinct. Only 3% of the secondary school children he surveyed do so "nearly every day" and 83% never do so. It would be interesting to know how many children are still put to bed with a "goodnight prayer". I suspect increasingly few. And even if they are, this is still a long way from the prayer of the biblical households in which they gathered as a community in clear relation to the whole covenant community. It is also a far cry from the practice of our forebears in this country until relatively recently. In his classic study of Anglican devotion C J Stranks noted that the "habit of family prayers, which the Puritans implanted, remained a cornerstone of religion until the revolution in family life which has occurred in our own day"(*Anglican Devotion*, London: SCM, 1961. p47). If Bible and tradition are not enough to convince us of the importance of family prayers, psychologists remind us how determinative the children's environment is on their formation. Common sense tells us as much. Indeed, in 1823 Henry Venn gave some sound advice to parents when he said, "children very soon and naturally conclude, that what their parents never mention, or earnestly inculcate, can be of little advantage to them" (*The Complete Duty of Man*, Derby: Henry Mozley, 1823. p226). John Keble was proof of the point the positive way round. To the end of his life he would say of all his benefits, "Why, I learned that from my father" ("Occasional Papers and Reviews", in Stanks, *Anglican Devotion*, London: SCM, 1961. p263). It is worth noting that Henry Venn's wife died when his children were quite young and so the responsibility for their development in the faith fell to him alone. Single-parent families may draw encouragement from him, as may those parents whose faith is not shared by their spouse. Family prayer in the latter situation clearly needs to be handled with a good deal of sensitivity but there are fruitful possibilities. Often a parent who does not claim to be a Christian, or at least, is not prepared to attend public worship, will be still very happy for the children to be nurtured in the faith and often want to be part of this process in the home. Indeed, I have known of fathers who have come to a living faith through praying with their children.

So how can *Celebrating Common Prayer* help a family to pray together? It can do so simply by offering a *root* and a *resource*.

A Root

Celebrating Common Prayer allows a family to root its prayer in the life of the Church. Traditionally, family prayers have had some connection with the liturgical life of the Church. This may have been simply reciting the Lord's Prayer, a practice which soon developed in the early church, or using the Books of Hours which became popular in the medieval church, or drawing on parts of *The Book of Common Prayer* for family devotions which became the practice of Anglican households from the seventeenth century onwards. To have some awareness that one's prayers are said in common with others, both in the parish and beyond, can strike a chord which is very deep. Children love to learn a short form of prayer or praise which they can relate to freely at home and find themselves joining in confidently with at church. Many parishes are trying to develop their community life, perhaps by experimenting with parish rules which bind the people together in some form of common life. Included in the rule will be some commitment to join in prayer at a certain time whether apart or together. *Celebrating Common Prayer* offers all sorts of opportunities to help churches as they try to root the prayers of their members in a common form, in words which will be shared by others well beyond their immediate life and in patterns which have been used by Christians throughout the centuries.

Perhaps because the Office is such a tried and tested way of prayer, it involves much which educationalists expect to find in activities which aim to engage the attention of children – and, indeed, adults as well. The Office which is *celebrated* rather than just *said* involves action, participation, interaction, repetition and short sequences of a varied input. Although it does not quite move with the same pace as children's television, it need not be a cerebral drudgery; and it will introduce some stillness into the day!

A Resource

Celebrating Common Prayer offers a resource to the family in all sorts of ways but especially by providing the Simple Celebration. The Simple Celebration is itself firmly rooted in the full form. It follows the same structure and keeps to the same flavour for each of the days as the full form, but it is shorter and very easy to use. It is preceded by a very helpful introduction which gives all sorts of advice on how to manage the prayer, including several tips for its use in the family. Before attempting to use the Simple Celebration with the family, it is worth reading this carefully, particularly reflecting on its advice that if it "is used as a form simply to be read through, it will not work: it depends on care being taken to make it true common worship". Think about your own family: the ages, needs, moods and movements of its members. The permutations are endless, but so are the possibilities. For me to prescribe would be to miss the point. A few principles are all that can be offered.

Be realistic   It is better to start off with a minimal commitment and build up from there than to bite off more than your family can chew.

Be adaptable   Your family is a unique and evolving community. Use as little or as much of the Office as is suitable, but try to keep to the basic pattern however much of a simplified form you are using.

Be embodied   There is so much scope for using movement and symbols in this sort of prayer. Remember that this is *celebration of prayer* and that bowing, raising hands, making the sign of the cross, kneeling and standing as well as using candles, icons and crosses will help your family in its experience and expression of prayer.

Be participative   Make sure everyone has a part to play. Young children may like to choose their favourite prayers, songs and Bible readings. Older children will want to read and there is no reason why the leading of the celebration should not be shared around the family.

Be musical   With the musical gifts of the family or with the help of a cassette recorder, try praising God in song together.

Be sensitive   Allow all that is happening in the life of the family to be brought into your time of prayer together and be prepared for the Spirit of Christ to touch and bless you.

Praying in other Informal Settings

Much of what has been said about family prayers applies equally to other contexts in which people gather to pray in an informal atmosphere. *Celebrating Common Prayer* is designed to provide a *root* and *resource* to help groups and individuals to pray in whatever context they find themselves. You may be the leader of an intercessory or contemplative prayer group. You may be a member of a house group in which prayer and praise take place as well as teaching and sharing. You may find yourself being asked to lead some prayers before a church meeting of some sort. You may be part of a parish worship committee thinking about ways of reviving your Sunday evening worship. You may be discovering that you are being led into times of solitude to pray alone for the needs of others. In all these circumstances, *Celebrating Common Prayer* will have something to offer.

When discussing ways of prayer, it is easy for people to place liturgical and free prayer at opposite ends of the spectrum and then go on to equate formality with one and informality with the other. However, any observer of the way groups pray can easily spot the order which develops, whether planned or unplanned, in the free form of prayer and can equally sense the free offering of prayer, perhaps being said in the heart rather than with the voice, in the liturgical form. Indeed, often in prayer meetings people ask for help to launch them into prayer and to direct them once there. And those involved in more structured praying also look for space to pray as the Spirit leads. The set and the free cannot be placed against each other as opposing alternatives. They meet in the dynamics of the group, the psychology of the individual and in the earliest experience of Christian prayer. When analysing the development of prayer in the first centuries of the Church, Geoffrey Cuming describes a pattern which included both extemporary freedom and liturgical order ("The First Three Centuries" in *The Study of Liturgy*, ed. Jones, Wainwright & Yarnold, London: SPCK, 1978. pp353–7).

It would be even more unfair to characterise liturgical prayer as formal and free prayer as informal. Some free prayer meetings can be very formal affairs, often with a stiff and cold atmosphere, and some occasions of liturgical prayer, particularly where there is familiarity and intimacy within the group, can feel very informal and relaxed.

The appeal which Taizé forms of prayer have amongst people from all sorts of traditions, and the growing popularity of prayers from the Iona Community, shows that the set and the free are two dimensions of the same reality. When they are allowed to coalesce with each other and complement one another by that third dimension which is made up of words which evoke, music which engages and leadership which sensitively guides the people at prayer, and when they are inspired by the fourth dimension of the Holy Spirit's presence and power, the set and the free become what they are meant to be: tools which help us to meet with God.

As with the family context, there is little point giving detailed advice about how *Celebrating Common Prayer* may help the business of prayer in all the various informal contexts we are considering. There are just too many variables for me to say much that would be useful. Besides, the fun is to be had in experimenting with the possibilities. However, three basic principles should be borne in mind by those preparing the time of prayer.

Community In whatever way you use *Celebrating Common Prayer*, remember that its aim is to help people pray as members of the whole Christian community.

Celebration Allow the time of prayer to be an event – a "happening", as people like to say today, and not just a catalogue of words to be recited.

Creativity Adapt to the particular community and context in which you find yourself but also keep that community's prayer in clear relation to the wider Christian community.

This may still all sound rather abstract, so here are some ideas on how *Celebrating Common Prayer* might be used in the context of an informal prayer meeting.

Make the room look inviting. It should be both relaxed and orderly, perhaps with the chairs arranged in a circle with a candle in the middle. Give out a copy of the Simple Celebration's Evening Prayer or devise your own similar version. After the usual welcome and introductions have a time of silence as you wait in God's presence.

Celebrate the coming of Christ amongst you as you begin with the opening responses and the lighting of the candle. Someone, whom you have asked beforehand, will then read the psalm, reflectively and carefully. Have some silence, to give space for the words to penetrate and be turned into prayer in the hearts of the people. If you want to use a canticle, that should follow now. It is concluded by a prayer. You could use the prayer which is provided or use this moment as a chance to offer your meeting to God and pray for the guidance of the Spirit.

After this the reading takes place. It would be good for the reader to stand as a sign of the importance of God's Word. Give the group time to reflect on the words of Scripture and allow people the opportunity to share how God may have spoken to them through the reading, perhaps calling to mind needs which should be prayed for later. Then lead into a response to the reading and a launch into prayer. You could sing a form of the *Magnificat*, or have some songs or a chant of some form.

It is now time for the intercessions. You could flow straight into them or you might want to break and discuss topics for prayer with the group. You could stay together as one group or you may prefer to split into smaller groups, each charged with their own areas for which to pray. If you remain as one group, try using the short *Kyrie* litany. This consists of verses from the psalms which have been made into prayers. In the Monday to Saturday forms there are three petitions. The first prays for the life of the Church, the second for those in special need and the third for the coming of God's Kingdom throughout the world. They could be used together as a beginning to the intercessions or individually as an introduction to each section of the prayers. As you enter the free prayer, encourage people to keep the "Lord have mercy" running throughout the prayers as a common ending and response to each one.

When it is time for the meeting to come to an end, use a collect as a way of summing up all the prayers and then draw people into one by saying the Lord's Prayer. Finish in a familiar way. If you had split into smaller groups bring people back into one group for these concluding prayers.

After the meeting make some notes on what worked and

95

what did not seem to work with your group. Next time put the lessons you have learnt into practice but persevere with the basic pattern and soon it will become familiar to people. The more familiar it becomes, the more effective it will be as a vehicle for the free offering of prayer.

Celebrating Common Prayer:
A Postscript

What is "Common Prayer"? For many people, it means any act of worship taking place within a given tradition — although that tradition is likely to be Anglican. The reason for such an identification derives from the name given to the standard Anglican service book — *The Book of Common Prayer*. Yet that title is only part of the story, for when the BCP was first published in 1549, it had (and it still theoretically has!) a much longer title, carefully put together in order to embrace all the different types of service envisaged in the Reformed Catholic Church of England. The first prayer book was entitled *The Book of Common Prayer* (meaning Morning and Evening Prayer, and the Litany) *and administration of the Sacraments* (meaning Baptism and Holy Communion) *and other rites and ceremonies of the Church* (meaning such services as confirmation and burial, as well as thanksgiving after childbirth, and even the Commination service on Ash Wednesday). Thus, although for many people, "common prayer" is a generic Anglican term for public worship in its carefully-regulated form, it is clear that for Archbishop Thomas Cranmer and his colleagues it had a narrower and more specific meaning. One might almost say that it had a polemical meaning. An explanation would be helpful at this point.

Most parish clergy and friars at the end of the Middle Ages used what was called a *breviary*, a book of Daily Offices with the seven services for each day. As far as we know, instead of being recited in seven small bits, they were frequently recited in two large chunks, in which the morning and the afternoon-evening services were merged together. It was convenient, neat, and offered the "duty" ("*officium*") to God. When I consider such a clericalised form of daily prayer, I am reminded of a motto I once heard from a French liturgist: "it is more important to say the Office than

97

to have said it." Perhaps it was this kind of motivation that made Cranmer wrench the daily prayer of the Church from the ranks of the clergy and monks, and hand it aggressively back to the whole community. For Cranmer, "common prayer" was not a kind of regimentation of all worship for all time – his enthusiasm for further revision in 1552 (and the rumours of yet more to come from him that circulated subsequently) certainly puts paid to that notion! "Common prayer" was rather a means of enabling a whole community, lay and ordained, to worship on a daily basis according to agreed and seemly conventions. Moreover, these conventions were likely to change with time and not fossilise.

The particular liturgical project which this small collection of essays has set out to elucidate can thus claim to stand firmly within the tradition of Cranmer's intentions. Indeed, one of the reasons for adopting the title *Celebrating Common Prayer* is to say in a twentieth-century mode exactly what the first prayer book proclaimed many years ago, namely that the daily prayer of the Church is too important to be left to the clergy on their own, and that it needs to be restored, once more, to the whole Christian community, wherever it meets. As these essays have shown, some of the particular presuppositions of the BCP Daily Offices do not stand up to the test of time or to the much better knowledge we now have of the worship of the early centuries, for example in the way the psalms are recited and the general approach to the use of Scripture. There is, also, a pastoral concern that the BCP Offices, at least in their definitive form in 1662, imposed a heavy burden on people, requiring them to meet invariably in church. One of the straightforward needs arising from the passing of time is, quite simply, a judicious flexibility.

The project draws in large measure from the forms of daily prayer that have appeared in recent Anglican revisions, notably that of *The Alternative Service Book 1980*. But it will be apparent that *Celebrating Common Prayer* moves further by taking the thinking behind recent revision to its logical conclusion. For example, instead of providing a "simple" and a "full" form of daily prayer, there is a more direct recognition of the fact that family prayer and formal group prayer are two distinct contexts for worship, requiring different approaches. Similarly, the kind of symbolism, with Bible, light, and even incense, or flowers, and balloons are seen to be ways of bringing a genuinely "folk" touch to a part of the worship of God that has been for too long repeatedly taken over by those who enjoy drudgery and derive satisfaction from finding the correct place for this or that antiphon in an obscure corner of a complex book. Cranmer's fight to hand "common prayer" back to the people of God has to be rejoined within the whole tradition of the Church Catholic but on the terrain of twentieth-century humanity. Much of that restoration lies not with the mere production of a book of texts but rather in the way those texts meet ever-new contexts, and find their own climate, their own ambience, their own house style. A book cannot, of itself, do this. It must come from imaginative use.

The group of people who have written these essays have all been involved in the production of *Celebrating Common Prayer*. In particular we all owe an enormous debt to David Stancliffe's vision in bringing us together in all our diversity to sit round a table and thrash out a common approach to this project. Saxton-Bampfylde, a firm of international business consultants based in Westminster, sponsored the project, provided the buildings in which we met, and fed us. Their involvement perhaps symbolises the unofficial character and lay orientation of our work. Anthony Saxton and Stephen Bampfylde are both heavily involved in their local parish churches, serving as churchwardens at different times. They are also boldly committed to the need for a spirituality that is both recognisably part of the tradition of the living Church and genuinely "lay" in its character.

It is thus very much up to people to take up what we have offered and test it out in the coming years.

There are some questions which have required careful consideration and judgment, such as which version of the

Psalter should be used and what kind of lectionary should be fashioned. In the end, we went for those we thought the best available, and which would win through into international acceptability. The Psalter is that which first appeared in the American *Book of Common Prayer* 1979. The Episcopal Church of the USA has continually made small alterations to the old Coverdale Psalter of the 16th century (the Psalter in the 1662 Prayer Book). From its own Prayer Books of 1789 right down to that of 1928, an increasing number of clarifications and substitutions of obscure or obsolete words have been made. The 1979 version, however, resulted from a fresh examination of the Hebrew texts, like other modern versions in the English-speaking world. The same is true of the Liturgical Psalter produced in 1977 by David Frost and Andrew Macintosh at the behest of the Church of England Liturgical Commission. There was a need to start afresh, on the basis of the original Hebrew – rather than work on Coverdale, which was (in effect) an English translation of a Latin translation of a Greek translation of the original! However, although the Frost-Macintosh translation was adopted by the Church of England Liturgical Commission, and bound with many editions of the ASB, freedom has always existed to use others, the old and much-loved Coverdale and the modern Grail Psalter included. Also the 1979 text has a style more in harmony with the Revised Standard Version of the Bible, which we have largely adopted for the new alternative canticles. Many Religious Communities on the basis of long experience of both the Frost-Macintosh and the new American BCP have indicated a strong preference for the 1979 Psalter because it is easier to recite and more rhythmical in style for the kind of reflective recitation required in many contexts. There are signs of its gradual adoption elsewhere in the Anglican Communion – and beyond. Anglicans, however, must not feel that they are tied to only *one* Psalter; it must be remembered that the Scottish Prayer Book of 1637 boldly adopted the Authorized Version's psalms, equally mellifluous as, but more accurate than Coverdale.

As far as the Lectionary is concerned, CCP has to make provision both for week-day and Sunday usage. In many places, the Roman Catholic Daily Eucharistic Lectionary is followed, even when the Eucharist is not celebrated every day of the week. On the other hand, the ASB Daily Office lectionary is a bulky affair when used in conjunction with the Daily eucharistic readings, and its long passages do not harmonise with the shape and style of daily prayer which we are trying to open up to the Church at large. A fresh approach was needed to this important ingredient of worship – hence the new provisions we have made. The Sunday readings, which do not have to be used where other practices are dictated by local liturgical patterns, are therefore of a different order. The ASB Sunday readings follow an adapted version of the 1967 lectionary of the British Joint Liturgical Group, which is a two-year scheme, and has a thematic flavour. Although it has been adopted in some other parts of the Anglican Communion, by far the more widespread is the Sunday lectionary produced by the Roman Catholic Church in 1969, which is a three-year scheme, in which (as far as possible) course-reading of certain books of the Bible is the norm. The American BCP made certain adaptations of this form of readings, as did other North American Churches, and ensuing collaboration at the ecumenical level has produced a number of improvements, resulting in the *Revised Common Lectionary* (1992). Recent work by the Liturgical Commission of the Church of England has made much use of these developments. In the end, we decided to opt for this truly international kind of lectionary, which sets the rich narrative quality of the biblical authors before the Christian community in a way that is both deeply traditional and thoroughly contemporary.

These decisions were taken corporately, and after much consultation. We worked, as well, in the inevitable sub-groups, balancing interest and background when aiming for different elements in the various services of prayer. Material, whether psalms, prayers, or readings, was constantly tested out, for example by Christopher Cocksworth at home with his family, or by Sarah and David Stancliffe on a pilgrimage walk from Le Puy to Compostela. Theological Colleges, Religious Houses, parishes rural, urban, and suburban (they have souls too) – all these played a part in the faith and practice that lie behind CCP. Without Brother Tristam's organising ability and eye for detail, the project would not have seen the light of day.

All liturgical books have a provisional character. Like a new building, their life is circumscribed from the very first day of issue. Moreover, liturgical revision is part of the life of the Christian community, a sometimes nervous compendium of tradition and renewal. We know that Cranmer relied for much of his liturgical work on the various unofficial "Primers" – books of prayers, psalms and canticles that were in circulation in the decades running up to the production of the first two Prayer Books in 1549 and 1552. To have such material in use meant that the ground for liturgical change was already being prepared. We hope that *Celebrating Common Prayer* will achieve a comparably prophetic and strategic place in the years that lead into the next century. We hope, too, that it will provide some needful stability, as the Church continues to assert the same need Thomas Cranmer articulated in deeply liturgical terms, namely to give "common prayer" back to the whole community, whoever and wherever they may be, as they offer the sacrifice of praise, "at all times and in all places", to the living God.

THE REVD DR KENNETH STEVENSON